Praise for *Fin*

M000040897

"Pasi Sahlberg, who introduced the world to the remarkable educational system in Finland, delineates four lessons that can be useful to educational leaders throughout the world. Sahlberg's clear, cogent, and conversational presentation is both powerful and timely."

—**Howard Gardner**
Author of *Truth, Beauty, and Goodness Reframed*

"About 25 years ago, two of us had a visiting scholar from Finland who wanted to know about cooperative learning. When he returned home he invited us to do workshops on the teachers' role in structuring cooperative learning and why it is effective in increasing achievement, building relationships in the classroom, and encouraging positive mental health. Several years later, a group of Minnesota legislators met with Pasi Sahlberg in Minneapolis where Pasi also invited us to attend. He turned to us and said that cooperative learning, as he writes in this book, was being used in every school in Finland. After reading this greatly important book we think we need to go back to Finland to see that ourselves."

—**David W. and Roger T. Johnson**
Professors of Education, University of Minnesota

"Pasi Sahlberg is probably the world's most knowledgeable scholar on across-the-globe education and teaching. Here he writes a primer on Finnish education, making clear that imported teaching and learning practices have greatly enhanced indigenous ones. The Finnish culture of inclusive leadership will give policymakers in many countries pause. They tutored me on leadership as culture while I was helping them borrow peer coaching—to my lasting benefit."

—**Bruce Joyce**
Author of *Models of Teaching*

(Continued)

(Continued)

"This short, wonderful book captures the essence of Finland's best education practices. Sahlberg clearly and compellingly describes simple steps to improve learning and teaching for all students. Every superintendent, school board member, principal, and teacher leader should read this book and follow its recommendations."

—**Tony Wagner**
Expert in Residence, Harvard University iLab and
Author of *The Global Achievement Gap* and
Creating Innovators

"Pasi Sahlberg, an original thinker and keen observer of schools worldwide, has done it again. In *FinnishED Leadership*, he builds on his best-selling *Finnish Lessons* with a lucid explication of the real leadership lessons we can take from Finland's schools. This book includes strategies that principals, teachers, and school leaders can pursue to advance recess as a student right, champion equity as the foundation of learning, implement the genuine lessons from Finnish schools instead of the urban legends, and encourage the use of small data as an antidote to quantification, correlation, and algorithms. *The Comenius Oath*, which begins, 'As a teacher I am engaged in educating the next generation, which is one of the most important human tasks,' makes the book worthwhile by itself. An engaging, powerful, and elegant read."

—**James Harvey**
Executive Director, National Superintendents Roundtable
Co-author of *The Superintendent's Fieldbook*

"As my state grapples with growing economic inequality and an aging and declining population, creating strong schools that support child well-being and nurture the capabilities of all of our children has become an imperative—not just for human dignity but also for sustainable economic prosperity. This book is less about Finland than about how education systems generally can engage in consistent development of human potential. Sahlberg's emphasis on well-being and on the essential value of educators' professional capital to systems improvement is a hopeful and refreshing break from failed narratives that have exacerbated equity challenges and incentivized narrow, test-focused instruction."

—**Rebecca Holcombe**
Secretary of Education, Vermont

"Every school system has its own unique strengths and weaknesses shaped by historic, political, and economic forces. Despite the success of the Finnish system, it is a mistake to emulate it in its entirety but rather, as Pasi Sahlberg points out in *FinnishED Leadership*, it makes more sense to pick out the Finnish strengths—a commitment to equity, valuing physical activity as a contributor to education success, and the use of small data—and apply those measures to your own unique system."

— **The Hon. Adrian Piccoli, MP**
Former New South Wales Minister for Education

"My takeaway of this book is how it busts some current myths about Finnish schools. Child-centered school that emphasizes physical activity in and out of classroom, equity, and authentic student assessments suggested in this book provide a good foundation for developing education for the 21st century. Inspired by Finnish educational leadership this book contains concrete and usable ideas for leaders working at different levels of education systems. *FinnishED Leadership* is like an excellent dinner spiced by author's insights of Finland's schools and finished by his international experience.

—**Peter Johnson, PhD**
Director of Education, City of Kokkola, Finland

"Pasi Sahlberg understands that school leadership is more than just increasing test scores but about creating the conditions for teaching and learning to promote happiness, curiosity, engagement, and collaboration. This new book is a must-read for all education leaders."

—**Jonathan Hasak**
Director of Public Policy and Government
Affairs at Year Up

FinnishED Leadership

Corwin Impact Leadership Series

Series Editor: Peter M. DeWitt

FinnishED Leadership

Four Big, Inexpensive Ideas to Transform Education

Pasi Sahlberg

CORWIN
A SAGE Publishing Company

A SAGE Publishing Company

FOR INFORMATION:

Corwin

A SAGE Company

2455 Teller Road

Thousand Oaks, California 91320

(800) 233-9936

www.corwin.com

SAGE Publications Ltd.

1 Oliver's Yard

55 City Road

London EC1Y 1SP

United Kingdom

SAGE Publications India Pvt. Ltd.

B 1/I 1 Mohan Cooperative Industrial Area

Mathura Road, New Delhi 110 044

India

SAGE Publications Asia-Pacific Pte. Ltd.

3 Church Street

#10-04 Samsung Hub

Singapore 049483

Executive Editor: Arnis Burvikovs

Senior Associate Editor: Desirée A. Bartlett

Editorial Assistant: Kaitlyn Irwin

Production Editor: Amy Joy Schroller

Copy Editor: Amy Marks

Typesetter: C&M Digitals (P) Ltd.

Proofreader: Dennis W. Webb

Indexer: Amy Murphy

Cover Designer: Michael Dubowe

Marketing Manager: Nicole Franks

Printed in the United States of America

ISBN 978-1-5063-2542-2

This book is printed on acid-free paper.

SUSTAINABLE FORESTRY INITIATIVE

Certified Chain of Custody

Promoting Sustainable Forestry

www.sfiprogram.org

SFI-01268

SFI label applies to text stock

17 18 19 20 21 10 9 8 7 6 5 4 3 2 1

Contents

For Otto and Noah

Preface

It's All About the Culture of
Educational Leadership

G reat leaders are also leading learners. If leaders don't learn, then the learning in the organizations they lead is not likely to flourish. Good learners take risks when they learn and try out new ways to do things better. This means that leading learners learn how to fail, learn from their mistakes, and continuously improve what they do based on their previous experiences.

What school leaders do reflects the values, beliefs, and cultures embedded in their schools. Leadership cultures in schools vary significantly from one country to another. Since the early 2000s, most of the efforts to explain Finland's educational success in international assessments have ignored or paid only marginal attention to educational leadership. I would argue, however, that Finland has a unique culture of leadership in general and of educational leadership in particular that deserves to be noted. The four ideas presented in this book are borne from Finland's brand of leadership culture in education.

FOUR IDEAS INSPIRED BY FINLAND

In recent years I have had numerous opportunities to host delegations of educators visiting Finland from the United States and other parts of the world. Most visitors return home thinking that they would like to test out in their home schools ideas inspired by Finnish schools. But there are others who think that Finland is too different to serve as a model. Reflecting on these responses inspired me to write this book.

I have often heard the question, "What can I do to incorporate some elements of Finnish education in my own leadership work?" Likewise, I have seen many examples of Finnish lessons applied in other countries. In Japan, I visited a primary school that had adopted the Finnish method of teaching reading (it was called the PISA method). In Italy, I saw schools using mathematics textbooks from Finland (in Finnish!) to teach mathematics (and Finnish) to primary school pupils. In the United Arab Emirates, I witnessed two schools employing Finnish-style pedagogies and school leadership. In the Dallas–Fort Worth, Texas, area of the United States, I saw school districts restructuring their schedules in order to increase time for all children to play outdoors and engage in physical activity during the school day. These initiatives have had various levels of success. Based on my observations and research, I have come to believe that educators who want to enjoy the level of educational success experienced in Finland should focus on four strategies in particular.

In addition to the four strategies presented in the four chapters of this book, it is important to understand that the book is grounded in two important arguments. First, *many influential theories, models, and ideas found in Finnish schools were originally formed in the United States by American educators and scholars.* Second, *there are many good practices and policies in Finland that, if implemented adequately, would significantly and permanently improve education quality and equity in other countries.* If this logic is right, then it follows that strategies need to fundamentally change from reform by innovation to development by better implementation.

The four ideas offered in this book are

1. Regular recess and physical exercise are crucial for substantial learning.

2. Small data can often be more effective than big data for achieving big changes.

3. Enhancing equity is an essential component of improving quality of education outcomes.

4. Adhering to myths about Finnish education can divert you from the path to improving your school.

This book is written to offer school leaders who work at the district, school, and classroom levels practical ideas and policy suggestions. Although there are many references to practices and policies in the United States, the ideas and strategies in this book can be useful in educational systems around the world. Whoever you are and wherever you test out these ideas—remember that to rush educational change is to ruin it.

Acknowledgments

It is great to be part of Corwin's Impact Leadership Series. First, I want to thank my publisher for making this book possible. Arnis Burvikovs, Desirée Bartlett, and Kaitlyn Irwin, you did a marvelous job. Thank you. I am also grateful to the series editor, Peter DeWitt, for asking me to join the team of writers and then guiding me during the writing process to get this book done.

I have received comments and support from several people for this book. I appreciate all of them. Special thanks to Sam Abrams, Jean-Claude Couture, and Sam Sellar for reading the entire manuscript and for your thoughtful comments and suggestions. You made this a better book and me a better writer.

Jonathan Hasak worked with me on the initial version of this book. I want to thank Jonathan for his contribution to the small data section. I truly enjoyed having lunch with George Pataki, thank you for giving me the reason to write this book.

Finally, I want to thank my family for their understanding, support, and love, especially when I was away from them to test my ideas in practice for this book. You are my inspiration, and you give me purpose to write and talk about improving the educational system. I dedicate this book to my youngest sons, Otto and Noah. Long may you run.

About the Author

 **Pasi Sahlberg**, PhD, started his career teaching mathematics and physics for six years in Helsinki Normal Lyceum, a teacher training school at the University of Helsinki in Finland. He often identifies that as the most interesting and important period in his long and broad career as an educator. He later taught science and mathematics education at the University of Helsinki; served almost a decade at Finland's National Board of Education, leading the national science education curriculum task force, the unit for teaching methods development; and advised on education policies and research related to the implementation of Finland's school reforms.

He started his international career in the 1990s as a consultant to the World Bank, the Organization for Economic Cooperation and Development (OECD), and the European Commission. In the early 2000s he moved to Washington, D.C., to join the World Bank's education team. His international career continued in Torino, Italy, with the European Training Foundation, before he became director general of the Center for International Mobility and Cooperation (CIMO) in Finland in 2009. From 2013 to 2016 he was a visiting professor at Harvard University's Graduate School of Education, where he taught international education policy and leadership.

In 2011 Pasi published his first international book, *Finnish Lessons: What the World Can Learn from Educational Change in Finland* (Teachers College Press), which immediately became a global best-seller. Now in its second edition, *Finnish Lessons* won the 2013 Grawemeyer Award and has been translated into 26 languages. He has contributed chapters to several education books and published over 100 research and professional articles on topics ranging from classroom teaching and learning to school leadership and international education reforms. His most recent books are *Hard Questions on Global Educational Change* (Teachers College Press), which he wrote with his students and teaching fellows at Harvard, and *Empowered Educators in Finland* (Jossey-Bass) with Karen Hammerness and Raisa Ahtiainen, which is part of a large research project, the International Teacher Policy Study, led by Professor Linda Darling-Hammond at Stanford University.

Pasi speaks around the world about educational change, leadership, and school improvement. He has addressed national parliaments in England, Scotland, Australia, and New Zealand, and has spoken before the European Parliament and the U.S. Congress. He has made more than 500 keynote presentations at large events (e.g., the International Confederation of Principals convention, the IB Heads Conference, and TEDxNewYork). He has also given guest lectures at Columbia, Vanderbilt, Stanford, and Harvard Universities and at King's College London, the University of Melbourne, the National Institute of Education in Singapore, and the University of Toronto.

Pasi's work in global education has been recognized by various awards and honors. He won the Finnish Education Award in 2012, the Robert Owen Award in Scotland (2014), and the Lego Prize in Denmark (2016). In 2017 he was awarded the Rockefeller Foundation's writing residency in Bellagio, Italy. Currently he serves as an advisor to several governments and education systems and as an expert to international organizations. For more about his work, visit pasisahlberg.com.

Prologue

Accidental Lunch

The road winding through the hills and forests of the northeastern United States reminded me of the countryside of Finland, where I spent my childhood. It was a beautiful morning in April 2015, and I had already traveled 100 miles since leaving my home in Cambridge, Massachusetts. Ernie, who had kindly offered me a ride that morning, was an experienced educator who led a nonprofit that works towards helping all young people in his community go to college. If this trip were taking place in my native Finland, we could have easily traveled miles and miles without saying anything to each other. But in America, silence in the car or at the dinner table is uncomfortable or can be considered impolite. Therefore, I bravely engaged in conversation about education in the United States with Ernie. Our opinions about education were often parallel but occasionally differed. Ernie thought firmly that every young person in the United States should have a college degree. My view was that some of them would probably be better off with high-quality vocational and technical education instead. My experience was that too much accountability for teachers and schools leads to unintended practices, but Ernie thought that, without such pressure on schools, some kids would not get a good education. I found it delightful to have a healthy debate with someone with such extensive experience in teaching and learning—we both thought it is good to disagree sometimes. In good conversations, differing opinions are often a key to learning more. Since coming to the United States, I have learned that it is indeed all right to disagree.

We were headed to an education conference in a small town in upstate New York, near the Canadian border. As we headed north, I thought, *Why has Canada, which in many ways is similar to the United States, been more successful in building an education system, from the early years of childhood to higher learning?* I was very familiar with the Canadian education system and knew that in Canada education is considered a public good and that education authorities are responsible for defending public school systems from market forces; therefore, the Canadian education system is more accessible, of better quality, and more equitable than the system in the United States. Although high school graduation rates in some parts of Canada are worryingly low, as they are in many parts of the United States, educational performance overall, including learning outcomes, equality of opportunity, and affordability of a college education, are in much better shape in Canada. I was surprised to learn that my co-traveler that morning knew very little about Canadian education. Before we could go deeper into this intriguing and important topic, the car navigation system suddenly announced, "Your destination is on your right." I thanked Ernie for the ride and enlightening conversation. He told me we'd meet later that evening.

I was scheduled to speak at this education conference, which brought together educators and business leaders from the United States and Europe to explore opportunities to better fit school education to the needs of the work world. I had researched this issue from both national and international perspectives when I was in the Finnish Ministry of Education and Culture, where we had created models for diversifying educational pathways and structures to improve young people's options for education and work. American audiences seemed to find examples and models from other education systems interesting—not necessarily because they would be directly applicable in their own work, but because learning about different ways of doing similar things raises questions about and helps improve their own practices.

We had arrived at the venue in the early afternoon, and I had an hour until my session would start. After a long car drive, having something to eat seemed like a good idea. The host of the conference kindly escorted me to the restaurant, where the conference guests had already had lunch. I had just sat down when the conference chair brought in another speaker who also wanted to grab lunch before the afternoon session started. I greeted the newcomer and welcomed him to join me. This tall gentleman, probably in his late 60s with a neat haircut and wearing an expensive suit and shiny shoes, sat down across from me. I introduced myself as an educator from Finland and a visiting professor teaching at Harvard's Graduate School of Education. My lunch companion introduced himself as George and told me that he owns a farm in the state and enjoys raising animals. Well, looking at his stylish attire, I thought, *That must be a big, productive farm!*

"What do you do for a living, George?" I asked, to make sure I knew with whom I was having lunch and would be speaking on the same stage later in the afternoon. "You must have another job besides running a farm," I added. "Well, yes, I was the governor of this state for three consecutive terms some years back," George said. Although I was not very knowledgeable about U.S. politics and politicians, I thought that this George next to me must be George Pataki, former governor of New York and a well-known politician nationwide. George Pataki had been a powerful figure in state and federal politics for quite some time. He had never lost an election and was rumored to be considering a run for president of the United States in 2016. I knew that since the states in the United States have the final word in educating their citizens, state governors have a lot of influence in state-level policies and often in national education reforms as well. George certainly must have a firm view about American education, especially if he aspired to live in the White House one day. As our lunch arrived, I decided to find out what he had to say.

THE SOLUTION TO IMPROVING EDUCATION IN AMERICA

"As a governor, you must have had a lot to do with education in your state, but what do you think about education in the United States?" I asked. Without pause, George expressed his concerns that because of the number of underperforming schools in the

United States, America was losing ground in its ability to compete globally. He went on to speak about the teachers in America and how the fundamental problem, as he sees it, is having so many bad teachers in public schools. The current system in the United States, according to George, protects underperforming teachers, which, he argued, has eroded the status of the teaching profession. Many talented young teachers change careers after realizing how bad many schools are. If parents had more choice to choose good schools for their kids, George concluded, American education would be much better off.

As I considered George's views about American schools, I thought that his was not a unique analysis of American public education. Then, without my asking, George offered his four-part fix for what in his view was an embarrassing situation for America. First, get rid of all bad teachers, which he claimed were the main reason for students' poor educational performance. Then, turn around failing public schools by handing them over to new operators who would run these schools more effectively than the public authorities. George told me that while he was governor, his state passed the strongest charter school bill in the United States: "We didn't have charter schools in New York before I was governor. Now we have a charter school program that works well." He said that there's enormous pressure to expand charter schools so as to create competition across America. Third, end Common Core, which encourages the adoption of national standards for all schools in the country. George was strongly against any national education standards imposed on the states; instead, each state should be allowed to come up with its own standards. Finally, rather than having a single national testing system imposed on students in every community, institute standardized testing, but not from Common Core; and establish school report cards that compare neighboring schools. George said he is all for standardized testing that would reflect the desires of the people of a community or a state, not Washington, D.C.

Tougher competition among schools, more choice for parents to decide where to send their kids to school, rigorous standardized testing to hold schools accountable for higher standards, and having the ability to fire bad teachers sounded like the ultimate solution to

George. I had heard similar remedies several times before at other events around the United States. Many states had selected all or some of these policies in their recent education reforms, hoping that the quality of teaching and learning would magically improve. George's analysis of the state of American education and how to improve it were so far from what I thought were the main challenges facing education in the United States that I hoped he would not ask for my opinion of his analysis and theory of change. But my wish was in vain.

George leaned toward me and asked, "You are from Finland and teach at Harvard, both known for their extraordinary educational quality and rigor. What do you think about American education?" For a moment I felt uncomfortable about talking about the issue. How could I challenge a person who had much more personal insight and longer political experience with education in the United States? Although I have visited hundreds of schools across the country, I felt uneasy opposing George's personal views. Then I remembered what my grandmother had always told me: "Avoid talking about the things that you don't understand."

This helped me to phrase my reply to George: "There are so many things I don't understand in American education that I would rather not answer your question, George." He turned to me and continued, "What is it that you don't understand in our education system?" *Now this is getting difficult,* I thought. George obviously is not going to let me go that easily. "Well," I said, "the thing that has really bothered me most in your education system during my time at Harvard and even before is why the American educational theories and models that have made many other countries' educa-tion systems flourish are not used in your state or federal education policies and reforms." I told George that when developing educa-tion reforms, Finland, as well as several other successful education systems worldwide, had relied heavily on educational knowledge, practices, and wisdom from the United States and less on their own research, innovation, and development. I added that what puzzles me even more is that these same innovations and ideas that have helped Finnish schools and children to succeed have not been part of national or state education policies and reforms in the

United States. I was happy with this answer. George was not. He seemed to be puzzled.

I was unsure whether my new companion got my point. Had Americans really been helping other education systems to improve while at the same time the performance of schools in the United States had stagnated or, as many believed, declined steadily compared to the rest of the world? Tellingly, George was not ready to accept that argument right away. He turned to me and said, "Could you give me an example of an American education innovation that has helped Finland's schools to improve but that we here in America have not used in consistent, system-wide ways?" "Sure," I said. "Let me tell you what we have done to help all kids to succeed."

THERE'S MORE THAN ONE KIND OF INTELLIGENCE

In the early 1980s, professor Howard Gardner was working at Harvard on a new theory of the human mind that differentiated intelligence into primarily sensory "modalities," rather than seeing intelligence as dominated by a single general ability. I told George that Howard Gardner, whom I had the pleasure to have as a colleague at Harvard and also as a friend now, thought that school education should aim at developing children's multiple intelligences and thereby help them reach vocational and academic goals that are appropriate to their particular spectrum of intelligences. Pupils who are guided to do so, Professor Gardner believed, feel more engaged and competent and therefore are more inclined to serve society in a constructive way. Gardner presented this new, game-changing idea in his book *Frames of Mind: The Theory of Multiple Intelligences* in 1983 (Gardner, 1983). Since then, this book has become well-known and much read in Finland by students and teachers as well.

I told George that educators and policymakers in Finland contended, just like Howard Gardner, that IQ tests and most standardized assessments used in schools focus mostly on logical and linguistic intelligence. Although many students function well in this environment, some do not. Finnish educators and administrators who were implementing a new school system in the 1980s and 1990s found Gardner's theory a perfect fit for the emerging Finnish system. The main premise was that students will be better served by a broader vision of education, whereby teachers use various teaching methods, pedagogies, and activities to reach all students, not just those who do well at linguistic and logical intelligence. Teacher education nationwide was aligned to the theory of multiple intelligences by challenging newly prepared teachers to find ways that "will work for this student learning this topic." I concluded to George, the main philosophy of school education in Finland is to individualize learning to suit each student, employ versatile methods of teaching and teach complex knowledge and skills in multiple ways, and accept that anyone can learn anything if appropriate methods and learning supports are available. Without Gardner's works and influence, Finland's international success in education would most likely never have happened.

George seemed to pay very close attention to everything I had said about this American theory that had lifted Finland's schools to new heights in just a couple of decades since the 1980s. He grabbed a piece of paper from his pocket and took a platinum-plated Montblanc pen from his chest pocket. He wrote Howard Gardner's name and the name of his theory on the paper. Now he looked even more disturbed than earlier. *Could it really be true that we have had the keys to better schooling here at home but that others are better at making them work*, I assumed George was asking himself at that moment.

COOPERATIVE LEARNING BENEFITS ALL STUDENTS

George wanted to know more: "Is there another example of an American innovation in education that we have ignored here in our systemic efforts to make schools better but that has worked in Finland?" he asked. Somehow I had been expecting this follow-up question based on the perplexity I saw on George's face while he listened to how the theory of multiple intelligences had changed the views of educators and policymakers outside of the United States. "Of course, George," I said, "the list of those successful ideas *'made in the U.S.A'* but used more abroad is long and growing." The following was my second example to George.

More than a century ago, American philosopher and educator John Dewey realized that children learn better when they work on real-life issues together in small groups than they do when taught in large classes by a teacher. Dewey, who worked at the University of Chicago, never saw his ideas about teaching and learning take wings at the whole-system level in the United States. Nevertheless, evidence from the Eight-Year Study (conducted by the Progressive Education Association between 1930 to 1942)—in which 30 high schools redesigned their curriculum and staff development—clearly revealed the power of Dewey's progressive models of schooling. It was the post–World War II arms race between the United States and the Eastern Bloc that shifted the focus of schooling from the ideal of educating active citizens for democracy to mastery and discovery of science, mathematics, and technology. The legacy of the progressive education movement led by Dewey and his disciples, however, led to the birth of what is now known as *cooperative learning.* It is an approach to pedagogy that consists of various educational theories and teaching methods. Cooperative learning aims to organize activities in schools and classrooms into academic and social learning experiences. Cooperative learning is much more than merely organizing students into small groups; it requires structuring positive interdependence within those small groups, meaning that individual group members succeed or fail together.

I then explained to George that cooperative learning was first and foremost researched and developed in the United States. Inspired by the thinking and works of Morton Deutsch, John Dewey, Kurt Lewin, Alice Miel, and Herbert Thelen, cooperative learning with its various techniques, methods, and principles is one of the greatest innovations in the world of education. Chief masterminds since the 1970s include David and Roger Johnson from the University of Minnesota, Elizabeth Cohen from Stanford University, Robert Slavin from Johns Hopkins University, and Spencer Kagan from the University of California, Berkeley (Sharan, 1999). Cooperative learning landed in Finland in the mid-1980s, when the Finns invited American researchers—including the Johnsons and Liz Cohen—to educate Finnish teachers and teacher educators on the principles and models of this innovative approach. Finland's educators and policymakers were convinced by the American research studies that demonstrated that cooperative learning, as a pedagogical approach, benefited all kinds of pupils and was applicable to a range of subject matter. The authorities in charge of national education reform in Finland during the early 1990s were so confident in the potential of cooperative learning to improve schools in Finland that it was included as one of the main educational principles in the national curriculum and all teacher education programs thereafter. Many educators in Finland contend that cooperative learning, which is genuinely an American innovation with components added by Yael and Shlomo Sharan in Israel, has had an essential role in turning Finnish schools into places of productive learning.

After I had provided this additional convincing episode of an American innovation that had enhanced the quality of learning in Finnish schools but was practiced only in some American schools and districts, George still seemed confused. He once again took out the pen and paper from his pocket and asked me to restate the professors who had been instrumental in creating this pedagogical innovation as well as their respective universities. George probably wondered how much all that research, which led to successful school practices in Finland and elsewhere, must have cost the American taxpayers (millions and more, probably) and how Finnish and other school systems had turned this research into practical solutions when education reform after reform in the United States had ignored them altogether. Even No Child Left Behind (which George had wholeheartedly supported) said nothing about kids having a spectrum of intelligences that were all equally important. That law was also silent about the power of cooperation as a means to improve teaching and learning in schools. Although I was ready to head to the conference hall, George seemed to want to know more: "This is very important. Could you please give me one more example that would illustrate how an American innovation has helped Finland's kids do so well in school that we here at home have undermined?"

I also thought that this was important. The politicians and authorities who were behind designing state and national education reforms needed to understand that the path to fixing American education is not one requiring more research and innovation, which tend to result in research and innovation that is ignored in the United States but used elsewhere to improve education. The smarter choice would be to examine and compare how other countries, such as Canada, the Netherlands, Singapore, Japan, and Finland, implemented these and other American ideas to improve education and, consequently, better educational performance.

Perhaps George would become a new champion of this thinking, which many American educators and some institutions have encouraged, instead of launching large, expensive new initiatives or passing legislation, such as No Child Left Behind (2002), Race to the Top (2009), and the Every Student Succeeds Act (2015). I decided to give George one more example that he could use to convince his friends and allies that America needs a new direction. I saw George as a potential beacon of common sense, which is an essential component of any successful school reform. Hence, my third example, which is described in the next section.

SCHOOLS WHERE BOTH TEACHERS *AND* STUDENTS LEARN

In the 1970s there was a common notion among those working on educational improvement that unless teachers are educated and trained to teach in different ways, the quality of schooling is not likely to get any better. Seymour Sarason, another great American mind left in the shadows in the United States but praised by many abroad, said to me when he visited Finland in 1995, "There's an assumption that schools are for students' learning. Well, why aren't they just as much for teachers' learning?" Research on teachers and educational change, however, has shown the ineffectiveness of staff development and professional learning for teachers. Analysis of staff development that focused on teaching methods and curriculum suggested that as few as 10 percent of those who took part in development activities implemented what they had learned. In the early 1980s in the United States, an innovation called *peer coaching* emerged from the research and development work of Beverly Showers and Bruce Joyce.

Peer coaching is a confidential process through which teachers (two or more) work together to reflect on their current teaching practices; refine, improve, and develop new skills; learn from one another; teach together in classrooms; and take part in school improvement together. Showers and Joyce (1996) recognized that changing the way teachers think about student learning and how they should teach students requires more than traditional lectures or seminars. They insisted that the transfer of new skills from staff development to classrooms must also include opportunities to practice new skills in safe environments, receive feedback from experts and colleagues, and have opportunities to rehearse these new teaching skills in their own classrooms with trusted colleagues. These ideas arrived in Finland in the mid-1980s, when education reform was focusing on diversifying teaching methods. Researchers, teacher-educators, and policymakers decided to adopt peer coaching as a fundamental principle for the new teacher education and school improvement program nationwide. Joyce, who visited Finland in the 1980s, told Finnish educators that teachers learn from one another while planning instruction, developing teaching materials, observing one another work with students in classrooms, and thinking together about the impact of their teaching on their students' learning. What the Finns needed to do was to make sure that initial teacher education provided a scientific and practical platform for all teachers to engage in peer coaching in their schools, and to schedule teachers' work in such a way that allowed them to work with their colleagues. Today, most educators and policymakers in Finland think that without the peer coaching model Finnish teachers would not have created the strong professional, collaborative culture of teaching and learning that today is regularly reported about Finnish education. In Finland and other high-performing countries, the teaching profession has more respected status than it does in most parts of the United States.

Once again, George listed all these ideas, details, and names on his notes and placed them carefully back in his chest pocket. The time for his conference speech was approaching, and he suggested we walk to the auditorium together. "If you ever make it all the way to 1600 Pennsylvania Avenue, George, give me a call, and I will help you to put these ideas forward in American schools," I said to him tongue in cheek. While we walked across the yard, I wondered if George would pull out his notes and speak about the need to invest more in implementing American ideas in education and stress the need for less innovation that would probably benefit others more than the schools in the United States. I thought that he might make a comment about the need to cure what John Merrow (2017) calls the American education establishment's and business community's *"addiction to reform,"* and the great heritage of American educational ideas and how his country is a world leader in research and development in education, including generating pedagogical innovation and solutions to make all schools succeed. American education experts and researchers advise governments worldwide and help schools to become successful, and Finland is no exception. Perhaps George would speak about the good news and the bad news in improving American education. The good news is that all the necessary knowledge and skills to move American public education forward and closer to where many politicians, business leaders, educators, and parents would like to see it already exist. The bad news is that there are so many social factors in the United States that complicate the improvement of educational performance: cultural diversity, disparities in how schools are funded, and widespread child poverty. In addition, the politics of education, which is primarily an issue decided in 50 states and by more than 14,000 school districts, prevents professionals from making good decisions for schools and teachers. I was excited to hear what George would say in his speech.

I decided to sit in the back of the auditorium so that George would feel free to speak his mind about education without feeling the need to seek my endorsement. He walked to the podium—confident, calm, and in some strange way glowing. I held my breath. George began by saying how education is the way to provide every American with opportunities to fulfill their dreams. I agreed. It was that way in Finland, too. What followed then was not what I had hoped to hear. George's speech was the same as his three-minute reply to my original question at the restaurant an hour earlier: He wanted to make American education stronger by having more competition and choice, removing bad teachers, closing down failing schools, and all sorts of heavy-handed tactics for children and teachers. Teachers must work harder, kids should study longer in and out of school, and authorities should exercise tougher punitive accountabilities on teachers and schools. He believed that if you push the system harder, it will move, and that more charter schools would be a great idea.

Not a word about international lessons from successful school systems. No credits to world-famous American educational innovations that have been shown to work and had led Finland, Canada, Singapore, and others to successful educational reforms. No pride of what his own country had accomplished in education. Howard Gardner, John Dewey, Elizabeth Cohen, Robert Slavin, and Bruce Joyce were just names on a piece of paper in his pocket. I thought that it is a pity how many politicians have such a narrow and technical view of education, compared to how we educators understand education and how to improve it in a comprehensive, systemic way.

My presentation later that afternoon touched on the things I had told George. I stressed the need to learn from one another about improving education regardless of the obvious differences between our countries. I warned the audience not to try to copy or imitate other education systems but to try to understand why they often do the same things very differently from their colleagues in other countries. I emphasized the fact that all well-performing education systems today have become that way by learning carefully from other countries, especially from the United States. I then spoke about four leadership ideas that are inspired by Finland—more recess in schools, leading by small data, better equity in education, and understanding the difference between myths and facts—that I think would help American schools to improve. For this book, I was asked to present these four examples to help others who would like to try something that is a proven practice and commonly used in Finland. The next chapters are about clear and important ideas that I believe can help you to improve your schools.

CHAPTER

1

Make Recess the Right of the Child

ost school leaders would agree that time is a critical element in schooling. Time is a limited yet renewable resource in education. Often, if you wish to do more of something in your school, you need to do less of something else. Teaching and learning schedules are already packed so full that it is difficult to add more activities into them. It is a common belief, especially among politicians and other noneducators, that if something in school doesn't work well, it is because too little time is spent on it.

I was once with a delegation of concerned mathematics teachers and mathematicians who were meeting with their state governor and his advisors in the United States to hand over their appeal to improve mathematics learning outcomes in junior high school. Their main rationale was that mathematics performance, especially among boys, had decreased and attitudes toward learning mathematics were rather negative among all youngsters. What this delegation was asking from the decision makers was to add an hour of mathematics to weekly schedules for all students. The governor listening to the delegation replied: "Why do you think asking children to do more of those things that they don't like and won't learn well anyway would do any good for their learning outcomes?" He closed the conversation by suggesting that perhaps pupils should have less exposure to mathematics and more to something that they really like and were interested in doing in school. Indeed, doing more of the same rarely leads to different results.

This episode could have happened in any other country because, in so many ways, education systems around the world are very similar. School curricula from one country to another have the same subjects and similar hierarchy—with reading literacy, mathematics, and science at the top of the list of important subjects, and music, arts, and physical activity typically at the bottom. School schedules in different countries are based on 45- to 55-minute lessons in which students study one subject at a time with one teacher in charge. Being a good student or a successful school is, more often than not, determined by how high or low test scores in reading literacy, mathematics, and science are without paying attention to students' learning and growth in other subjects or other aspects of education.

TEACHERS AND STUDENTS NEED A BREAK

When we take a closer look at policies and philosophies behind visible practices in schools and classrooms, significant differences between school systems can be seen. One difference is how much time teachers and students are expected to spend in teaching and learning in school. Let's take a look at the role that time plays in typical public schools in the United States and in Finland. According to the data from the Organization for Economic Cooperation and Development (OECD) international database (OECD, 2016a) and from national statistics from the United States (Abrams, 2016) and Finland (Sahlberg, 2015), teachers in U.S. schools spend at least

25 percent more time teaching students compared to their peers in Finland. Identifying reliable and exactly comparable data about teachers' working and teaching time in the two countries presents some difficulties, but it is fair to say that American teachers spend one to two hours more every day in classrooms or in other ways instructing their students than do teachers in Finnish schools.

Another way to look at how time is spent in the United States and in Finland is to see how much time students spend on compulsory instruction. Although there are no entirely reliable data about students' compulsory or intended instructional time in these countries, OECD (2016a) data suggest that students in primary and junior high schools in the United States spend roughly 1,000 hours annually in various kinds of classroom activities, whereas that figure in Finland ranges from 660 hours in primary school to about 900 hours in middle school. These numbers translate to about 5.5 daily hours of schooling in the United States and from 3.5 to 4.7 hours a day in Finland. It seems, however, that more teaching hours and instructional time are not associated with better outcomes of education. In fact, including all OECD countries in this analysis reveals that there is no (positive) correlation between how long students' school days are and how much they learn during them (OECD, 2016a, 2016b).

Indeed, extended instructional time, for example, over the summer holidays, is not necessarily a good idea if the intention is to help all children learn better. Longer school days may be justified in some other ways but not by expecting happier and better educated children as an outcome. Study after study (see Shumaker, 2016) has also shown that increasing time for homework rarely leads to improved learning outcomes. An interesting aspect of Finland's school system is the relatively modest amount of time that students and teachers spend in school while still accomplishing fairly good results with modest spending. The same is true for homework in Finland.

HOW MUCH HOMEWORK IS OPTIMAL?

Although there are deeply rooted myths in the world about the absence of homework in the lives of Finnish children, the truth is that homework does exist, but in most cases it doesn't have the same central role that it has in many schools in the United States. If you ask primary school students in Finland about how much time, on average, it takes for them to prepare for the next school day, you will hear anything from 0 to 30 minutes. According to different surveys on schools and anecdotal evidence provided by teachers, students in junior high school in Finland typically spend about half an hour completing their homework. High school students' homework loads can exceed several hours a day depending on how many courses students take at any given time, because the modular structure of high school in Finland allows significant variations in students' work loads (Sahlberg, 2015). When I talk about homework in the United States with teachers, parents, and especially with students, I often hear much higher figures than those in Finland. Having a two-hour homework standard in the United States is not rare. Private tutoring and homework play central roles in high-scoring Southeast Asian countries—South Korea, Japan, China, Singapore, and others—but much of the rest of the world has reasonable practices regarding what students are expected to do outside their lessons in school.

SHOULD RECESS BE MANDATORY?

Where is this all leading, you may wonder. Experiences from Finland and some other high-performing school systems that have instructional time requirements for their students that are lower than the international average invite a question: Are we asking children to do too much, too fast in our schools? Maybe there is a balance between formal instruction in classrooms and unstructured time to play during the school day that triggers student learning and well-being. I think the biggest difference between the cultures of schools in the United States and in Finland is the pace of students' and teachers' daily lives in school. I have visited numerous schools in different parts of the United States and seen students rushing from one class to another because of the short amount of time allowed for between-class transitions. Teachers are equally busy, shifting from one lesson plan to another without a "pit stop" in the teachers' lounge because they lack an appropriate break. I have also noted that more schools than before have either reduced recess or have no recess at all anymore.

The United Nations Standards of Human Rights recommends that prisoners have at least one hour of outdoor exercise daily. This sounds like a reasonable right, regardless of the reason for imprisonment. I think we should give the same right to all our children. In some states now—Tennessee, most recently—legislatures are taking away requirements for daily unstructured play for children in school. In 2016 in the United States, only 13 states had laws that mandate recess time during the school day, and 8 had recommendations for physical activity in schools. Most of the U.S. states, however, have *NO* general physical activity requirement and *NO* policy requiring or recommending recess or physical activity breaks. Therefore, I suggest that American schools would greatly benefit if they considered Finland's recess model and adapted it for their schools instead of reducing summer holidays, lengthening school days, or adding homework for children. Some parents might be concerned that their children will fall even farther behind other children if classroom instruction time is decreased to allow more time for outdoor play. But the loss of effective learning time should not be an issue: Teachers and students in the United States spend significantly more time teaching and learning than their peers in Finland or in most other countries. Part of the current scheduled instructional time could be spent on something that has proven to have a positive impact on children: unstructured outdoor time for children and at the same time professional reflection time for teachers. But what is the evidence for that, you may ask?

Ironically, some of the most convincing research on the power of play has been done in the United States, at the same time that politicians and bureaucrats have been reducing recess time and play in and out of school. Children's museums (e.g., White, 2013), children's hospitals (e.g., Bickham, Kavanaugh, Alden, & Rich,

2015), academics (e.g., American Academy of Pediatrics, 2013), philanthropic foundations (e.g., Robert Wood Johnson Foundation, 2007; Lego Foundation, 2013), and research journals (e.g., *American Journal of Play*) are good examples of advocates for and evidence providers of the importance of recess and play for children's learning and development. A general finding in all of these studies and reviews is that recess and time to play benefit children's learning in school (in all subjects); enhance their social and emotional development; and are positively associated with their being more creative, more self-confident, less bullied, and more attentive in school.

Equally important, a wealth of published literature describes how physical activity improves children's health and mental well-being. A policy statement issued by the American Academy of Pediatrics (2013) concluded that "cognitive processing and academic performance depend on regular breaks from concentrated classroom work. This applies equally to adolescents and to younger children. To be effective, the frequency and duration of breaks should be sufficient to allow the student to mentally decompress." In Finland, this recommendation has been taken to heart for decades. Let's see how.

RECESS AS A REGULATION IN FINLAND

The Law on Education in Finland defines instructional time by stipulating that at least 45 minutes of every school hour must be allocated for teaching. In practice, the law is implemented in such a way that a lesson is 45 minutes long followed by a 15-minute recess. If schools decide to have longer lessons (e.g., 60 minutes or 75 minutes), then time for recess must be lengthened accordingly. Local municipalities and individual schools have a lot of autonomy to determine their daily schedules. Therefore, there is no universal model of a daily timetable for learning and recess in Finland. The law provides a general regulation that provides all children with a right to recess breaks in school. Figure 1 is an example of a typical school-day schedule for fifth graders (pupils who are about 11 or 12 years old) in Finland.

Figure 1 Example of a Typical Fifth-Grade School Day in Finland

Children in Finnish primary schools always go out for recess, rain or shine. In our fifth-grade school-day example in Figure 1, students have at least 60 minutes of recess during the day. In most schools, recess time is unstructured; it is up to the children to decide what they want to do. Some of them take a walk around the schoolyard with friends, while others play football (soccer) or other games. There are always those who prefer to chat with a friend or simply have a moment of solitude to arrange their emotions or thoughts. There are clear house rules for recess in every school, often prepared in partnership with children and parents, or at least agreed-to by them. At least two teachers must always be present in the school-yard to watch over the children. Recess in Finnish schools is considered as essential learning time, not a waste of time. Real learning often happens in fresh air, during physical activity, while having conversations with others, or simply because of an opportunity to concentrate on understanding previous lessons.

When visiting schools in the United States that do not have recess, one of the concerns I often hear from teachers and principals is for the security and safety of children. What if something happens in the schoolyard during breaks? This very question came up during a visit of an education delegation from the United States to Helsinki. One day I took this group of superintendents, school principals, teachers, and education experts to see what the recess culture in Finnish primary schools looks like. We were standing in the schoolyard with the school principal when the school doors slammed open and about 300 kids aged 7 to 13 ran out to have their awaited break outdoors. A boy, probably a fifth grader, passed us by running toward the schoolyard's far corner, which was full of trees and benches to sit on. He climbed up one of the trees, like a small monkey would, and sat on a branch some 10 or 12 feet high. The American school principal who had been watching the boy seemed to become worried when the boy reached his obviously frequently visited spot of the tree: "What happens if that boy falls down from the tree?" she asked. "He probably wouldn't do that again," said the Finnish principal. In this and many other schools in Finland, teachers tolerate a fair amount of risks when children play or engage in physical activity, certainly more than seems to be the case in the United States. "We provide all the safety that is necessary but not all safety that is possible to our children in school while they play," I heard teachers in the school say when they explained the culture of recess to their guests.

UNSTRUCTURED OUTDOOR PLAY BENEFITS WELL-BEING AND LEARNING

The importance of outdoor play and physical activity for children's health and learning is widely recognized in Finland and often confirmed by research from the United States (see box). Many of us, including me, need to move to think. There is no better way to enhance learning than to run and play in fresh air after or prior to a lesson that requires cognitive attention and deeper thinking. We also know from research that children's brains work better when they move. An experienced Finnish teacher put it this way: "Not only do they concentrate better in class, but they are more successful at negotiating, socializing, building teams and friendships together" (Doyle, 2017). Numerous research studies conducted in the United States (e.g., Howie & Pate, 2012) and in Finland (e.g., Syväoja et al., 2012) confirm the benefits of unstructured outdoor play and physical activity on children's well-being, health, and academic achievement in school.

More Time to Play in School

The LiiNK Project,[1] led by Debbie Rhea of Texas Christian University (TCU) in Fort Worth, Texas, aims to develop the whole child through increased recess and character development. The project now includes 20 schools that have been testing restructured daily schedules to provide students with more recess time. Rhea realized during her time in Finland that all schools allocate 15 minutes of each hour to recess so that children have time for unstructured outdoor play. Her point of entry into this project was the realization that schools have been cutting back on

(Continued)

(Continued)

breaks to squeeze in more instructional time in the classroom, believing it improves academic performance. Studies have revealed, however, that students are fidgeting, failing to stay on task, or zoning out completely.

Research in Finland shows that children who engage in more physical activity and have time to play during the school day do better academically than children who are sedentary. Inspired by the Finnish experience, the LiiNK Project provides Texas and Oklahoma students with four 15-minute recess breaks each day—two before lunch and two after. These students also take part in "Positive Action," a character-building curriculum taught three times a week. Results have been promising. LiiNK students were more disciplined and focused in the classroom, and they demonstrated social growth and development through a change in peer interactions. Off-task behaviors like fidgeting decreased by 25 percent compared to the control-school students. Students' academic performance on reading and mathematics also improved significantly. The character-building curriculum reduced discipline issues and bullying, increased respect for self and others, improved honesty and self-concept, and heightened students' sense of school-connectedness.

"Instead of coming home exhausted and watching TV or playing video games, parents reported that their kids were out riding bikes and playing with other kids," said Rhea in an interview recently (Shape America, 2017). During my visit to Fort Worth to see the impact of LiiNK Project, I heard from teachers how students with more outdoor play were motivated to complete their homework sooner than before. This is what has been done in Finland for a long time. It is not rocket science. It involves understanding who children are and what they need in order to feel good and do well in school. Rhea told me, "Change is hard when numbers don't tell the story—emotions do."

1. See the LiiNK Project website at https://liinkproject.tcu.edu.

Ten years ago, Google decided to encourage its engineers to use up to 20 percent of their working time on something related to what the firm does and about which they are passionate. The assumption behind this revolutionary idea was that innovation would have more space in a culture in which people have time to dig deeper in their own minds, interests, and curiosity. Gmail and Google News are results of what free-ranging engineers and scientists can invent when they follow this 20-percent rule. Many companies have since imitated Google by allowing their workers to take time to focus on their passions, in the hopes that this would improve performance.

Finland's recess policy in K–12 schools is an educational adaptation of Google's 20-percent rule—or, rather, Google's 20-percent leadership idea imitates Finland's primary schools' recess practice because Finnish schools have been allocating 20 percent of their total daily time to recess since long before Google was born. Indeed, in every Finnish school, students can spend one-fifth of their school day on things that they think are good for them. Finland's recess model also provides all teachers with the same advantage: Teachers have 15 minutes of every hour for their own activities. In most schools, teachers meet in teachers' lounges to chat with colleagues, drink a cup of coffee, or get ready for the next class. I argue that this simple idea of giving students and teachers time between lessons to rest their minds and brains helps them to think deeper, broader, and bolder when they get back to their core tasks—to learn and to teach.

Andy Hargreaves, one of the world's leading thinkers and an activist in educational leadership, has argued that we are now in transition between two eras of educational thinking that are very distinct from one another. The current era that we are just exiting, he says, is defined by increased effort for higher achievements, delivering faster and performing more cheaply. Performance standards, attainment targets, and international student assessments that are used to create global education league tables have been manifestations of this period, which started around the year 2000. The emerging new period is defined by a focus on students' well-being, engagement, and identity, Hargreaves says. At the same time, increasing obesity, type 2 diabetes, bullying in and out of cyberspace, and trauma caused by unrest, violence, and migration globally will be more present in our schools than ever before. This new period that we are entering requires different approaches to schooling, both in the United States and in Finland. If we are serious about children's well-being and health, then we need to change what we expect them to do in school every day.

Ways to Move Forward

Next I offer concrete ideas inspired by practices and policies in Finland to enhance well-being, engagement, and performance of people and schools through recess and physical activity, using the 20-percent rule. These ideas are targeted at three levels of leadership: system leaders (state, district, or school-cluster level), principals (school level), and teachers (classroom level).

1. *System leaders: Pave the way to a new culture of recess*

    Rethink the role of recess in schools based on research about the benefits of unstructured outdoor play and physical activity. Come up with a strong argument why more recess and outdoor play embedded in every day in school is good for all children. Recognize the health risks related to increased seat time in school and at home, which is often compounded by the increase in "screen time" among teenagers. Help your community and school board members to understand how increasing the narrow focus on academic work for long periods of time is backfiring, while at the same time the benefits of physical activity and play are often ignored when schools are seeking ways to improve. Become a champion of a "10,000 Steps a Day" campaign in your district, to encourage every student and every teacher to move at least 10,000 steps every day. Order safety inspections of playground equipment and facilities at regular intervals. Pave the way to a new culture of recess and keep in mind that when children play, quality is as important as quantity.

2. *Principals: Redesign your daily schedules*

    Work with your district and board members to get their support for a year-long experiment with increased recess time. Be bold and do what your colleagues in Finland do:

Give your students and teachers fifteen-minute breaks between their lessons. No less. Then make a collective effort with parents, students, and teachers to speak up in support of recess, and work with your community and school board to make sure playgrounds are safe and well-equipped. Have clear rules for the use of digital devices in school, especially during recess. Invite children to think about how to have more physical activity in school every day. Protect the role of arts and music in your school curriculum, because these programs often support what children do during recess. Volunteer to help supervise recess whenever you can. Recruit people from your community to supervise recess: Schools benefit from extra eyes on the playground. Remember that recess quality, not just quantity, counts.

3. *Teachers: Make recess time a learning time*

Help children to learn how to reenergize their brains and their bodies so that they can be attentive, learn, and achieve in school. Teach them these self-regulation skills and remind them how these skills are keys to living a happy and healthy life. Make recess part of learning in school, not something that has no value. Make sure students have clothes and shoes that are suitable for outdoor play. In primary schools, teach your pupils games that all children can take part in so that everyone is active and feels included at recess. Accept that some students prefer solitude every now and then. Mobilize your PTA or PTO to raise funds to buy new equipment and maintain the old. Recess quality improves when the playground improves.

CHAPTER
2

Use Small Data for Big Change

One feature that distinguishes schools in the United States from those in Finland and in much of the rest of the world is the adornment of classrooms, hallways, and teachers' lounges with data walls, which typically use brightly colored charts, tables, and graphs to display students' and classes' levels of performance on standardized tests. For some education reformers, such displays promote transparency: By revealing more information about schools, such data walls become part of the foundation for bringing about effective school improvement. Other reformers who are focused on improving school performance have pointed out, however, that these data sets don't necessarily spark insight about the fundamental realities of teaching and learning in classrooms. Rather, they are primarily based on analytics and statistics, not on the relationships and emotional dynamics that drive learning in schools. Confined to reporting quantifiable outputs and outcomes, they are inadequate instruments to capture and assess the impacts of learning on the lives and minds of students.

After the No Child Left Behind Act became U.S. law in 2002, states were required to administer standardized tests in reading and mathematics to all students in Grades 3 through 8 each year, and a single test thereafter for all high school students. Additionally, states were required to institute their own testing standards to hold schools and teachers accountable. In response to data from these tests, various teacher evaluation procedures have emerged. Despite all of these good intentions, more data are now available than can reasonably be consumed, and there has been no significant improvement in outcomes.

Increasingly, leaders of schools and education systems place importance on collecting, storing, analyzing, and communicating information about schools, teachers, and students based on these growing data sets. This information is commonly referred to as *big data*, a term that first appeared around 2000, signifying data sets that are so large and complex that processing them by conventional data processing applications isn't possible. Two decades ago the type of data processed by education management systems consisted of input factors such as student enrollments, teacher characteristics, or education expenditures handled by the education department's statistical officer. Today, however, big data covers a range of indicators about teaching and learning processes, and increasingly reports on student achievement trends over the long term.

To deal with this outpouring of data, international organizations continue to build regional and global data banks. Whether it's the United Nations, the World Bank, the European Commission, or the OECD, today's international reformers are collecting and handling more data about human development than ever before. Beyond government and nonprofit agencies, there are global education and consulting enterprises like Pearson and McKinsey that see huge business opportunities in big data markets in education.

We are indeed entering the era of digital-technology-mediated learning environments in education. With this revolution comes the promise that big data will lead to more powerful personalized learning, active student-centered pedagogies, responsive formative assessments, and increased overall efficiency in education. In any event, big data in education leads, whether purposefully or incidentally, to a recording of activity and interactions that provides large amounts of analyzable data in digitally mediated educational environments. This then requires new forms of data skills, especially syntheses and presentations, which has led to the emergence of two new fields: educational data mining and learning analytics.

DATA MINING AND LEARNING ANALYTICS

Educational data mining focuses on interpreting evidence from large amounts of noisy and unstructured data; for example, correlations between student behavior and learning. It answers questions like "What sequence of study is the most effective for a specific student?" and "Which actions indicate student engagement and satisfaction?" *Learning analytics* is more concerned with applying tools and techniques of larger scale in educational settings, in response to questions like "When is a student at risk of failing the course?" and "What grade is a student likely to receive without intervention?" Many education leaders today, especially in the United States, are engaged in hearing and reading about the new tools that come with new learning sciences.

Big data and algorithms (rules for using these data to find a solution to a problem in a finite number of steps) have already shaped many areas of conventionally human-dominated work. R. Martin Chavez, chief financial officer at Goldman Sachs, spoke at ComputeFest 2017 at Harvard University Science Center about how his institution has been shaken by big data. He said that, in 2000, Goldman Sachs had 600 humans making markets in U.S. stocks. By comparison, he added, "Today, we have two people and a lot of software" (Chavez, 2017). Today, one in three Goldman

Sachs employees is an engineer. The future of financial industry lies in smart machines, not in people anymore. There are those who predict that similar trends will occur in health care, elder care, and also in education. "Schools will diminish but education will flourish when robots and machines will take the roles of teachers," a speaker at Finland's 2017 Education Fair EDUCA argued. Online programs in many universities have already done that when algorithms calculate the best strategies for students to make the grade.

By definition, big data offers more versatile information about teaching and learning situations, which can be used to tailor more personalized learning solutions for students. Big data in education also opens new doors to researchers. Perhaps its greatest value, as Bill Cope and Mary Kalantzis (2016, 11) conclude in their article "Big Data Comes to Schools," is "the possibility in any particular case to analyze a variety of data types using a variety of methods, cross-validating these against each other in a more powerfully holistic, evidence-based repertoire of research practices." At the same time, however, we must be mindful of the potential drawbacks of big data, especially those related to data privacy and research ethics. When big data is used to determine children's educational pathways and their future, or to influence teachers' careers in education, we are entering a world in which questions of privacy, ethics, and a lack of humanity in decisions that affect people's lives must be taken very seriously.

CORRELATION IS NOT CAUSATION

Among the best-known international testing programs today is the OECD's Programme for International Student Assessment (PISA), which measures reading, mathematical, and scientific literacies of 15 year olds in the OECD countries and around the world (Sellar, Thompson, & Rutkowski, 2017). The OECD now also administers Education GPS, a global positioning system that aims to tell policymakers where their education systems place in a global grid, in other words, how different aspects of their education system performance compare to those of other education systems. Similar to the way GPS operates in your car, this OECD data system promises to indicate how to move to desired destinations in improving education. Although some observers would argue that PISA is not really big data because it is just a few hundred megabytes of data that are collected slowly and analyzed using traditional applications like SPSS, OECD's PISA chief Andreas Schleicher (2013) has called it that. Whatever the interpretation of PISA, the OECD has become a world leader in the system-level big-data movement in global education, but not everybody (Sahlberg & Hargreaves, 2015) agrees that this movement will be beneficial to schools and children in long run.

Despite all this new information and the benefits that come with it, there are clear handicaps in how big data has been used in education reforms. In fact, pundits and policymakers often forget that big data, at best, only reveals correlations between variables in education, not causality. As any introductory statistics course will teach you, correlation does not imply causation. Data from PISA, for example, suggest that the highest performing education systems are those that combine quality with equity (OECD, 2016b). This statement expresses the idea that student achievement (quality) and equity (strength of the relationship between student achievement and family background) of these outcomes happen at the same time in education systems. It doesn't mean, however, that one variable causes the other. Correlation is a valuable part of evidence in education policymaking, but it must be proved to be real and then all possible causative relationships must be carefully explored.

The problem is that education policymakers around the world are now reforming their education systems through correlations and algorithms based on big data from their own national student assessment systems and international education databases without adequately understanding the details that make a difference in schools. A doctoral thesis at the University of Cambridge in 2015, for example, concluded that most OECD countries that take part in the PISA survey have made changes in their education policies based primarily on PISA data in order to improve their performance in future PISA tests (Breakspear, 2015). But are changes based on big data really well-suited for improving teaching and learning in schools and classrooms?

FINDING THE HUMANITY IN THE DATA

It is becoming evident that big data alone won't be able to fix education systems (Sahlberg & Hasak, 2016). Decision makers need to gain a better understanding of what good teaching is and how it leads to better learning in schools. This is where information about details, relationships, and narratives in schools becomes important. These are what Martin Lindstrom (2016) calls *small data*: tiny clues that reveal big trends. In education, these small clues are often hidden in the invisible fabric of schools. Understanding this fabric must become a priority for improving education.

Small data emerges from the notion that in the world of big data we need different information about the events we try to understand. Small data is being used in designing new marketing strategies for companies at risk of losing clients, helping them to understand better the nuances of human behavior. In health care, small data is seen as a potential new portal to healthier living, as a way to avoid an exclusive reliance on correlations and predictions by large statistical medical data sets. According to some health experts, small data offers new solutions to challenges caused by an increasing focus on outcomes-based reimbursement models in health care. As we better understand what it means to be healthy in a more holistic way, this new focus on transitional care is about small—not big—data.

Education systems in many parts of the world today are becoming "governed by numbers" that originate from various kinds of studies, surveys, inspections, and standardized measurements about systems performance. To properly understand what makes students learn well or why some students struggle with learning, we also need small data that teachers and principals collect using different means in their schools every day.

In education the notion of small data is actually nothing new. Good teaching and learning in schools have always been based on teachers' and students' punctual and purposeful observations, assessments, and reflections of what is happening during teaching and learning processes in schools. Now, at the dawn of a new *education data science,* in which computers could support the analysis of organized complexities in education, it is becoming increasingly important to enhance the attitudes and skills related to small data in both educational research and practice in schools. My view of good education is based on collective human judgment that is supported by a variety of evidence from practice—both quantitative and qualitative (see box). From the school leadership point of view, it may be true that *if you don't lead by small data, you will be led by big data.*

Leading With Small Data in Mind

Adrian Piccoli was the minister of education of New South Wales (NSW) in Australia from April 2011 until the end of January 2017. His leadership philosophy is different from that of most other education ministers I know: He spent a significant part of his time in the field visiting schools and communities instead of sitting in his office in Sydney. His rationale was to learn to understand what happens in schools and then use these data as supporting evidence in policymaking. And to do that, he often went to sit among children in classrooms to be part of the teaching and learning process.

I spent a week recently with Minister Piccoli on a field trip in northeastern NSW. In classroom after classroom, he took a seat with the children—often on the floor with them—and listened to what they were saying, watched what the teacher was doing, and sensed the spirit in the classroom. At the end of that week, I told Piccoli that what he does as a system-level leader is an excellent example of what small data looks like in practice. By doing this, he said, he will be able to create a much deeper and personal picture of the complex fabric of education than would be possible from reading progress reports or spreadsheets alone. Just as IKEA's former CEO Ingvar Kamprad found that sitting behind a cash register was the best customer research (described later in the chapter), so was being part of a learning community with schoolchildren the best form of evidence for Piccoli to enhance the quality of, and equity in, education.

Piccoli, a fearless defender of more equitable school education in Australia, puts "kids before politics." He has no magic solution to leadership:

(Continued)

(Continued)

> There is no great trick to it. It's about listening to every point of view and sticking to facts and evidence. We never make up policy because it "sounds like a good idea." Everything we do is based on evidence, data and advice from experts, particularly teachers and principals. I also like to triangulate the advice I receive. That is, I rarely take the advice of just one person or group, or the department or Board of Studies, Teaching and Education Standards for that matter. I test their advice with practitioners to make sure it will work in the classroom. One of my mantras is that "if an idea doesn't work in schools then it doesn't work." (Quarry, 2017)

This is an example of small data in action at the level of top educational leadership.

A RENEWED FOCUS ON TEACHER-COLLECTED EVIDENCE

There has been a notable shift worldwide during the past decade or so from teacher-collected evidence through classroom-based assessments toward digital-technology-mediated data. At the same time, the role and use of standardized tests have become central in collecting these data. Teachers now spend more time in analyzing these data and trying to make sense of what the results would mean in their own work with students. I am not saying that this is necessarily a bad thing. But if teachers become steered primarily or exclusively by external data from standardized knowledge tests and inspection reports, the effect would be to undermine the complexities of teaching and learning in schools.

SMALL DATA AND FINNISH EDUCATIONAL LEADERSHIP

There are school systems where sources of information much broader than numbers and statistics from standardized tests are analyzed and used to guide the work of the schools. In Finland, for example, a central element of monitoring the work of a school is a *student welfare team* that consists of teachers, health specialists, counselors, and members of school leadership. Student welfare teams meet regularly, in most schools weekly, focusing on individual students to discuss and process information brought in by teachers concerning their students' well-being, behavior, and learning in school. Through these small data, gathered collectively first-hand, early interventions are then selected and implemented to help students at risk.

Finland's education system does not have any census-based external standardized assessments that would test all students regularly in core subjects (often limited to reading literacy and mathematics). The only external standardized test for Finnish students is the matriculation examination at the exit from high school. This examination serves primarily the purpose of assessing the maturity of high school graduates for college and university education. Examination data are not used for accountability or quality assurance purposes at all, although the news media often report the results of annual examinations and rank high schools based on those data.

The absence of national census-based data about students' achievement in Finland requires that alternative forms of assessments and data be systematically used for monitoring, reporting, and policy development purposes. This is where small data comes into the picture in Finland.

Sample-Based Assessments on a Wide Range of School Subjects

First, politicians and authorities rely on sample-based national assessments in holding the system and its units (schools, principals, and teachers) accountable for results. These sample-based assessments are employed on the basis of multiannual education assessment plans approved by national education authorities. They cover a much wider range of subjects and areas of schooling than just reading literacy, mathematics, and science.

Evaluation at the Local Level

Second, local authorities in municipalities (or districts) are required by law to regularly evaluate and monitor what schools do and whether they accomplish expected outcomes. Since there is no one streamlined national standard or procedure for local education evaluation, practices vary from one municipality to another. Sometimes larger municipalities have common benchmark tests for all their schools and students to make sure that all schools are adequately on board with achieving the goals set in municipal curricula. In other municipalities, all schools have their own school-made forms of assessing educational performance and progress.

Assessment at the Classroom Level

Third, a significant part of teachers' work and professional responsibilities includes various kinds of evaluation and assessments, for instance, student achievement, progress of individual students, identification of special educational needs and support, as well as teachers' own professional growth and development. Initial teacher education, therefore, contains studies that focus on understanding and being able to design and manage all these different forms of assessments.

Tiny Clues About How Students Learn

Small data in Finland plays an important role as part of the evidence pool that teachers, principals, and local authorities use when they collectively judge the performance of education in their schools and communities. Big data that comes from national sample-based assessments, national and international surveys, and international student assessments complement locally collected data. Small data in education is about phenomena and events that are occurring at the transactional level of an individual student, teacher, classroom, or school in real time. These data are used in a timely, insightful, and actionable way at the point of teaching, learning, and leading, wherever that may be—from the classroom to the community.

Martin Lindstrom (2016), the author of *Small Data: The Tiny Clues That Uncover Huge Trends,* tells a story about his meeting with the founder and then-CEO of IKEA, Ingvar Kamprad. At the reception desk of the Stockholm headquarters of this global furniture giant, Lindstrom asked where he might find the boss. The answer was that he was either in his top-floor office or at the cash register in IKEA's store downstairs. Lindstrom found Kamprad at what appeared to be his rather usual workplace, serving clients behind one of the store's many cash registers. Afterward, when they were having a conversation about leadership and strategies behind IKEA's huge global success, Lindstrom asked why the CEO takes time from his busy schedule to serve customers when that could be done by a cashier or even a machine. The answer was that there was no better way to understand why clients buy certain items instead of something else, or why they choose IKEA rather than one of their many competitors in town. For Lindstrom this was an ideal example of a leader's instinct and the power of small data in driving success. Virgin's Sir Richard Branson and Fiat Group's Sergio Marchionne are other living examples of highly successful business leaders who have relied on raw instinct and small data in building their successes.

Small Data in Classrooms

The main difference between big and small data in education is, of course, the size of data and how these data are collected and used. Big data in education always requires dedicated devices for collecting massive amount of noisy data, such as specific hardware and software to capture students' facial expressions, movements in class, eye movements while on task, body postures, classroom talk, and interaction with others. Small data relies primarily on observations and recordings made by human beings. In education these include students' self-assessments, teachers' participatory notes on the learning process, external school surveys, and observations made of teaching and learning situations through peer coaching, for example.

Teachers have a key role in collecting and using small data in schools. They understand better than anybody else their students—their characteristics, needs, and potentials. Teachers in Finland have strong executive control of planning, teaching, and assessing in their work.

In many education systems today, teachers' roles in curriculum planning and assessing students' performance have been diminishing. Teachers often teach predetermined curricula and follow preapproved instructional scripts. Their students' learning and their own effectiveness as teachers are judged by external criteria and data.

Another necessary condition for expanding the role of small data as part of teachers' professional repertoire is for teachers to have enough time to do this. In the United States, as we saw in Chapter 1, teachers at all levels of schooling spend more time daily in classrooms than their peers in Finland. It is therefore understandable that when teachers in American schools are asked to do anything that is above and beyond what they already do, a common complaint is that there is no time for that. Teachers can make better use of small data and thereby improve the quality of teaching only if they have more time to work with their colleagues every day as part of their regular work.

Here is an example of the role of small data from my own work. I taught mathematics and science for many years in a combined junior high and high school in Helsinki. Like so many of my colleagues around the world, I soon realized that there are many students who don't find these subjects interesting. Although many young people recognize the importance of math and science, they find these subjects too remote from everyday life and form no personal connection with them. Early in my career I learned that many students, probably most of them, have self-constructed ideas of scientific and mathematical concepts and phenomena. These students' private ideas are difficult to capture except by turning those ideas into tangible representations, such as stories, drawings, or conversations.

I invested a lot of time back then in collecting small data (although I didn't call it that) to understand students' own ideas about mathematical and scientific worlds. In science classes, for example, I tried to find out what my students thought about the concepts we were about to study. Gravity, electricity, and planetary motions are concepts about which students often have constructed their own ideas through experience, often in conflict with the ideas they study in class. Research shows that students' self-made ideas of scientific concepts or mathematical laws, however erroneous, are often very difficult to change, even by the best teachers. A key point here is that standardized test data cannot inform a teacher about these important hidden cognitive forces. Rather, it is small data that can help teachers to understand why some students don't learn as well as they could in schools.

In a research study John Berry and I conducted in Finland and England in the early 2000s, we were particularly interested in exploring what mathematicians look like through the eyes of school-aged children. If we knew that, we argued, we could also better understand children's own beliefs about mathematics as a subject and what their relationships with it might be. In our study we asked children what they saw when they thought about mathematicians at work. We collected the data by asking children to draw an image of a mathematician.

Figure 2 A Student's Image of a Mathematician

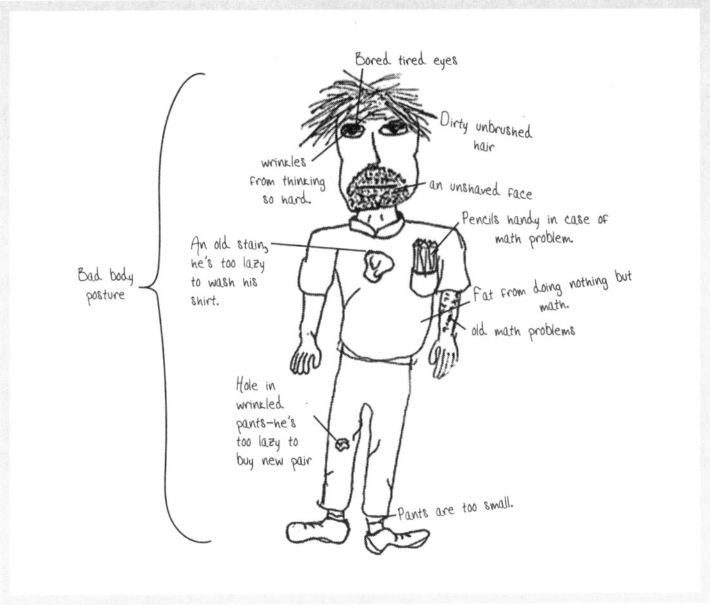

Source: Sahlberg & Berry, 2003.

Figure 2 illustrates a common image that students have of a mathematician. As well as drawing a picture, pupils were asked to write a description of their image. The pupil who drew Figure 2 wrote that "mathematicians have no friends (except other mathematicians), are not married or seeing anyone, are usually fat, are very unstylish, have wrinkles in the forehead from thinking so hard, have no social life whatsoever, are 30 years old, and have a very short temper" (Sahlberg & Berry, 2003). It is easy to conclude that anyone having a vivid image of a mathematician like this probably wouldn't be very interested in learning mathematics or be excited to consider becoming one when they grow up. My point here is that if we continue to ignore the power of students' own ideas and conceptions, we will only perpetuate the notion that mathematics and science (among other subjects in our school curricula) are irrelevant, uninteresting, and difficult to learn. Furthermore, the potential of small data for helping both teachers and students to understand these misconceptions and images is one prospective way forward in improving the quality of education.

Ways to Move Forward

Following are three concrete recommendations inspired by practices and policies in Finland to enhance the use of small data in the work of schools:

1. *System leaders: Make room for alternative assessments and authentic data*

   Reduce census-based system-level student assessments to the necessary minimum and transfer saved resources, including time, to enhance the quality of formative assessments in schools and school-based alternative assessments. Emphasize school improvement rather than testing and measurements by creating conditions for all schools to engage in peer reviews that pave the way to deeper collaboration and professional learning. Ensure that all teacher education programs and teacher licensing procedures include well-defined elements of modern knowledge and skills required to employ locally managed assessments, including small data. Support smart use of formative and other school-based assessments, because evidence shows that they are more likely to improve the quality of education than conventional standardized tests. Revisit current professional standards for teachers and school leaders and ensure that they pay proper attention to evaluation and assessment as essential aspects of the work of educators in all schools.

2. *Principals: Strengthen collective autonomy*

Strengthen collective autonomy of schools by giving teachers more independence from bureaucracy and simultaneously investing in teamwork in your school. This enhances social capital that is proved to be a critical aspect of building trust within education and enhancing student learning. Build trust in your school because it is perhaps the single most needed ingredient missing in education systems today.

3. *Teachers: Find out students' own ideas and beliefs*

Empower your students by involving them in assessing and reflecting on their own learning and then incorporate that information into collective human judgment about teaching and learning (supported by national big data). Because there are different ways students can be smart in schools, no one way of measuring student achievement will reveal success. Students' voices about their own ideas and growth may provide those tiny clues that can uncover important trends for improving learning.

Toward Better Data

Big data is commonly believed to be transforming the way we think, work, and live. For many of us this is an optimistic promise, whereas for others it creates anxiety and concern regarding control and privacy. Big data is often defined to encompass the four Vs: volume, velocity, variety, and veracity of information. I see small data in education as encompassing four dimensions: timely, purposeful, formative, and collective.

1. **Timely:** Small data is transactional in nature, and there is very little delay between getting the information and acting on it. (For example, my student's emotional state is "perplexed." Will this affect how he will be able to engage in learning?)

2. **Purposeful:** Small data represents pertinent information that directly affects teacher performance and student learning in school. (For example, do my students understand what they already know about the topic at hand, and are they aware of related beliefs?)

3. **Formative:** Small data can be predictive of possible learning difficulties and poor outcomes. (For example, are critical aspects of home support lacking that could jeopardize my student's success?)

4. **Collective:** Small data is coherent across the school and collected by all school personnel. (Are we making collective human judgments that are informed by evidence about my students' behaviors and performance in school?)

W. Edwards Deming once said that "without data you're just another person with an opinion." But Deming couldn't have imagined the size and speed of today's data systems. Automation that relies on continuously gathered data is now changing our daily lives. Drivers today don't need to know how to use maps when they can use smart navigators that find them the best routes; airline pilots spend more time flying on autopilot than by hand. Political election campaigns are steered by big data, and failures of those defeated in elections are explained by the lack of small data: In the United States, some observers have argued, Barack Obama won in 2012 because of his campaign's use of small data and Hillary Clinton lost in 2016 because her campaign was relying too much on big data. Similar trends are happening in education systems, with countless reformers trying to "disrupt" schools as they are.

In general, politicians don't trust educators. As a consequence, there is a lack of public trust in teachers who, in turn, then don't trust their students. This is a vicious circle of distrust in today's education. Experience suggests that trust in people and in institutions can be built only by genuine deeds that give them more responsibility and agency. In Finland, trust in schools and education in general began to flourish soon after the government allowed schools to design their own curricula (steered by a national framework curriculum), to evaluate the effectiveness of their own work, to control their budgets, and to professionalize the middle-level leadership. Ceremonial speeches and political appeals have had diminishing impact on changing the culture of education in this respect. When schools have real ownership and responsibility for small data, professionalism in schools will be enhanced. That is one of the conditions that must be in place before trust in our teachers will start to grow.

Big data has certainly proved useful for global education reform by informing us about correlations that occurred in the past. But to improve teaching and learning, it behooves reformers to pay more attention to small data—to the diversity and beauty that exists in every classroom—and the causation they reveal in the present. As with many other things in life, the ideal solution for sustainable improvement of education is a mature combination of big data and small data. One thing seems certain: If you don't start leading through small data, you will be led by big data and spurious correlations.

CHAPTER

3

Enhance Equity in Education

K allahti Comprehensive School is a typical suburban public
school in Helsinki, Finland. Kallahti serves 560 students from
Grades 1 to 9, more than 45 percent of whom are from immigrant-
background homes. The school is the workplace for 55 teachers, 6
of whom are special education teachers. I went to visit the school
because I wanted to find out how this school serves children who
have special educational needs. While there, I visited three special
education classes, each with 10 students, each led by a special education teacher and supported by one or two trained assistants
(there were four assistant teachers in this school). I also learned
that 38 other students with varying special needs were integrated
in regular classes at the school, and assisted by an expert teacher.
The school curriculum that teachers and administrators have
designed for their school promises a special focus on ensuring that
all students have access to a good education and individualized

help whenever needed. Dropping out or repeating a grade is not an option at Kallahti.

Kallahti is not an exceptional school in Finland. Equality of educational opportunity has been the centerpiece of Finland's education policies and national education reforms since the early 1970s, another example of an American idea imported to help build a successful school system in Finland. The Finnish Dream, as I call it in my book *Finnish Lessons 2.0: What Can the World Learn from Educational Change in Finland?* (Sahlberg, 2015), was to have a good neighborhood school for all children, regardless of family background, community characteristics, or personal conditions. Guaranteed access to a good primary school that has properly educated personnel was an imperative that addressed both human rights and economic concerns in Finland at that time. Finland was a small agrarian and relatively poor nation, and educating every child equally well was the best option for social cohesion, democracy, and prosperity. The Finns paid close attention to the conclusions of the 1966 Coleman study, "Equality of Educational Opportunity," which found that students' academic achievement was less related to the quality of a school, and more related to the social composition of the school and the students' family background. Finnish educators and politicians concluded that if schools influence children's educational pathways and prospects in their later lives, then schools must be prepared to cope with inequalities that children bring with them to school every day. All schools should be able to address in a systematic manner the health, nutrition, and well-being of every student together with educational disparities caused by differences in socioeconomic status.

EQUALITY OR EQUITY

Equality in education often refers to equal rights to a quality education (access) or equal treatment of girls and boys in school (gender equality). People sometimes think that equity means that we give all students the same education and then expect them to reach the same targets. This was a common perception of equity in

Figure 3 Equality Is Not Equity in Education

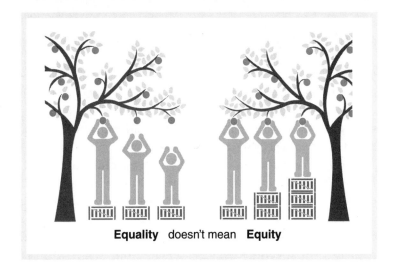

Equality doesn't mean **Equity**

Finland for a long time following the school reform launched in the 1970s. Rather, equity in education is about *fairness* and *inclusion*. Fairness means that personal or social circumstances such as gender, ethnic origin, or family background are not obstacles to achieving educational potential. Inclusion, in turn, ensures that all children in school reach at least a basic minimum level of knowledge and skills. Better equity in education therefore means that all differences in educational outcomes are not the result of differences in wealth, income, power, or possessions—in other words, home background (see box).

Equity is measured in the international student assessments by calculating the strength of the relationship between a student's measured achievements (in reading, mathematics, and science) and her or his home background. According to the latest OECD PISA study, Finnish students were among the top performers in reading literacy, mathematics, and science, and in Finland, socioeconomic background had one of the weakest impacts on student learning among the OECD countries (OECD, 2016b). Many visitors to Finland and analysts of its schools have been intrigued by the fairness and inclusiveness of the Finnish education system.

FINLAND'S STRATEGY FOR EQUITY

Enhancing equity has been the driving principle in Finland's education system development since the 1970s. Even today the national education policy priority is to combat widening achievement gaps—between pupils, between schools, and between communities—and thereby secure system-wide equity. There have been two distinct periods in enhancing equity in education in Finland. First, in the 1970s and 1980s there was strict central steering and external control of schools. Prescribed state curricula and syllabi, school inspections, and detailed state regulations of must-dos and do-nots gave the government a strong grip over what happened in schools. Central control required, among other things, that all schools have comprehensive health services, healthy school meals, and early intervention support free of charge for children who needed them. Equity was ensured through laws, equalizing funding and regulations passed by the central government.

During the second period, which started in the early 1990s, a devolution of authority to local communities increased school autonomy. Schools took responsibility for curriculum planning, student assessment, school improvement, and self-inspection in their schools. School inspections were replaced by self-evaluations, peer reviews, and individualized professional support; fiscal control moved to the municipalities and in many cases to schools; and a sample-based student assessment system was strengthened to help monitor the overall performance of the Finnish education system without schools fearing being ranked or forced to compete with one another. A critical aspect of the transformation of education governance was a school-based, teacher-made curriculum. The new system standards required that each municipality create its own curriculum, including descriptions of school values, a mission statement, and the overarching goals of education. Since this transformation of the education system, schools have become the central places where curriculum planning takes place.

How an American
School Enhances Equity

After visiting Faubion School of Portland, Oregon, in early 2017, I found it to be a good example of what one school can do to enhance equity. Faubion is a learning site for 550 students in pre-kindergarten to eighth grade in northeastern Portland's Concordia community. About 80 percent of these students live in poverty and up to one-fourth are homeless or housing insecure. Faubion's next-door neighbor is Concordia University, a private nonprofit Christian liberal arts university with a strong focus on preparing teachers for primary schools. When LaShawn Lee became the new principal of Faubion in 2008, she walked into Concordia's College of Education and asked what the school and the college could do together to help children. While their interaction over the years ebbed and flowed, this was truly the start for what some observers call a new model of American education—collaboration between public school and private college.

The new Faubion School + Concordia University, a "3 to PhD Community" building that is jointly funded by Portland Public Schools and Concordia University will bring the school and the college physically together: most College of Education faculty will reside in the school to make interaction even easier, and school teachers will have access to the facilities of the college. As I walked around the construction site with the school's new principal, Jen McCalley, she said: "This is a very unique arrangement. We have researched the United States and have not found anything quite like this yet." I also spoke to Concordia University Foundation's chief development officer, Kevin Matheny, who told me that "when new students come to our college, they should not wait for a couple of years to see a classroom. They're going to be right in the middle of a real school setting and from day one they're going to learn what teaching in school is all about." The concept of a partnership between a teacher-education institution and a school is similar to Finland's teacher-training school model, although the academic program structure in these two countries is very different (Hammerness, Ahtiainen, & Sahlberg, 2017).

I was impressed to see how Faubion School and Concordia University were collectively committed to enhancing equity of

(Continued)

education and teaching quality with support from their "3 to PhD" initiative that aims to create safer, healthier, and more educated communities from early learning through pursuing one's highest dreams. This new education model that strengthens health, well-being, early learning, and more sustainable educational improvement resonates closely with the spirit of the Finnish model of schooling.

TWO WAYS TO EQUITY

Over the course of decades, two strategies have enhanced the equity of schooling in Finland: (1) school-based, teacher-made curriculum and (2) teachers' and school principals' access to continuous professional learning and development.

Local Control

School-based curriculum gives teachers and administrators the power to define values, purpose, and overall educational goals for their school. Teachers and principals rely on their own professional judgment, the views of parents and the community, and evidence from surveys and research. The terminology and style of school curricula in Finland are very down-to-earth, reflecting the moral aspects of education rather than the political rhetoric typical of government-created policy documents. Our Finnish experience shows that if we allow schools to formulate the details of what is important in education, they typically say things like "everybody has the opportunity to succeed" and "all pupils have access to good learning" in ways that are possible to accomplish in practice. Common to the mission statements of Finnish schools is a strong emphasis on equity in schooling, that is, ensuring that pupils' home backgrounds don't determine their school performances. School-based curricula are, therefore, an important strategy to convert system-level equity policies into concrete actions and structures within schools. When teachers work to ensure that every student succeeds, it often means much more than when legislators sign and act with the same intention.

Access to Ongoing Professional Learning

Access to continuous professional learning and development helps schools improve their work toward their equity goals. Just like medical doctors or engineers, educators must update their knowledge and skills to build professional capital throughout their careers (Hargreaves & Fullan, 2012). The Finnish government has maintained professional learning and development as one of its policy priorities since the start of the era of stronger school autonomy in the early 1990s. Each year the state budget allocates some US$30 million to teachers' and principals' professional learning and development. Municipalities that provide most of the funding for schools also invest in continuous improvements for their schools. Professional development and school improvement are based on the demand and needs of schools and, therefore, focus primarily on implementation of the schools' own curricula. Finnish teachers and administrators have, on average, seven days of professional learning and development each year. Half of that time is their personal time out of working hours. By taking this approach, Finland spends 30 times more funds on the professional learning and development of educators than on accountability procedures, including testing students and surveying schools. In testing-intensive education systems like in the United States, this ratio is the other way around.

EQUITY IS CENTRAL TO SCHOOL IMPROVEMENT

When schools emphasize equity, this emphasis redefines the meaning of *school performance*. Standardized testing has become the most common way in the United States and in many other countries to measure school performance. Test-based accountability relies on data from these externally mandated standardized tests. Teachers and school principals are then held accountable for their students' learning based on these data. Finland is different in this respect. An absence of standardized tests leaves schools responsible for assessing student achievement. A high-performing school in Finland is one where *all* students perform beyond expectations (that may mean different things for different students). In other words, the greater the equity and resiliency, the better the school is regarded in Finland.

An education system that is equitable and in which students learn well redresses the effect of broader social and economic inequalities. When I speak about equity in education, some people wonder why Finns think that this is important. My answer is that inequity in education systems demonstrates a failure to utilize fully students' cognitive and personal potentials. Small nations like Finland cannot afford to leave any child behind. Increasing numbers of refugee children and others who were not born in Finland underline the importance of equity in education policy. We know from our own statistics that more equitable education is also cost-beneficial in long run.

The OECD (2012, 2016b) has concluded that the highest-performing education systems across OECD nations are those that combine quality with equity. Other research (e.g., Heckman, 2011) demonstrates that investing as early as possible in high-quality education for all students, and directing additional resources toward the most disadvantaged students as early as possible, is a cost-effective strategy that will produce the greatest impact on improving overall academic performance.

Many observers believe that Finland's special education system is one of those key factors that explain Finland's world-class results in achievement and equity in recent international studies of school systems. My personal experience, based on working with and visiting hundreds of Finnish schools, is that most schools pay particular attention to those children who need more help than other students in becoming successful. This was my impression of Kallahti Comprehensive School; it is a good example of a Finnish school with a strong focus on equity through early intervention and individualized support to children. Many U.S. teachers and administrators I know think the same way but are often stuck in the middle of *excellence versus equity* quandaries due to external demands and regulations. In my view, standardized testing that compares individuals to statistical averages, competition that leaves weaker students behind, and merit-based pay for teachers all jeopardize schools' efforts to enhance equity. None of these factors exist in the Finnish education system.

MARKET FORCES DO NOT IMPROVE SCHOOLS

School-choice advocates in the United States—former New York governor George Pataki and Secretary of Education Betsy DeVos among them—believe that the introduction of market mechanisms allows equal access to high-quality schooling for all and that such market mechanisms will thereby improve the quality of education. These same people also think that charter schools will unlock educational innovation and enhance access to better schools for more American children. However, evidence does not support these views, as the OECD and American research have shown repeatedly (Abrams, 2016; OECD, 2016b; Tucker, 2012). School choice and associated market mechanisms often lead to segregation of children and schools. Chile and Sweden are examples of education systems where market-based school choice through vouchers and privatization has been a primary policy, ahead of enhancing equity and supporting children and schools with special needs. These case studies and systematic research on them have shown that when equity of outcomes decreases, so does the quality of education (Adamson, Åstrand, & Darling-Hammond, 2016).

Let me stress that the United States and Finland are very different nations, as are their education systems. Finland has no private schools for which parents pay tuition, with the exception of one school, the International School of Helsinki, which largely serves the children of international diplomats and businesspeople. Education reform in Finland has intended to make all public schools good places for children to learn and teachers to teach. Indeed, education in Finland—from early years to adulthood—is seen as a public good that eventually benefits the entire society. It is difficult to have an equitable education system that has market-based school-choice policies because choice invariably increases school inequality and segregation.

Finland has followed the path of fairness and inclusion in building a more equitable school system. Linda Darling-Hammond (2010) has made that appeal for American education in her award-winning book *The Flat World and Education*. Suggestions that Darling-Hammond (2010) made to enhance education equity in the United States are parallel to the policies employed in Finland since the 1970s. Finland has invested fairly and more heavily in schools within disadvantaged communities and insisted that the best way to provide equal educational opportunities for all is through public schools.

Ways to Move Forward

I next suggest some concrete actions inspired by policies and practices in Finland to enhance equity and thereby improve the quality of American schools.

1. *System leaders: Make education funding fair and needs-based*
   Ensure that finance policy and school budgeting focus on equitable resources and their cost-effective use. Schools should receive their budgets based on the kinds of children they serve, not on headcount or the wealth of the neighborhood where the students live. Introduce policies that attract qualified and experienced teachers to teach in high-needs schools. Prioritize special needs education resources, both personnel and money, to schools that serve more diverse populations of children and homes. Design equivalent high school vocational pathways for students as alternatives to dropping out. Strengthen well-being and health services in all schools, for all children, every day of the school year. Work actively with colleagues in charge of other public sectors and community partners to expand high-quality early childhood education and care to all children (especially to those living

in underprivileged families). Increase schools' engagement and responsibility in curriculum planning, with a particular focus on enhancing equity of education in schools. Design a system-wide action plan to strengthen equity of outcomes in all schools.

2. *Principals: Improve conditions for shared responsibility*
Ensure that teachers and teaching teams have the time, knowledge, and educational resources to develop methods and differentiate instruction to meet the needs of each student and support each student's well-being, growth, and learning. Strengthen the culture of shared responsibility along with individual accountability in your school by insisting that all school personnel understand the educational and personal requirements of equity. Provide your teachers with opportunities for peer coaching as a support mechanism for their professional learning and development. Lessen the role of standardized tests to the necessary minimum and compensate that with the systematic use of small data. Avoid early tracking of students based on academic ability. Promote further inclusiveness, early intervention, and preventive care as the main strategy in your school and ensure that there are enough special education teachers and assistants.

3. *Teachers: Teach through the whole-child approach*
Ensure that each child in your classrooms and in your school is healthy, safe, engaged, supported, and appropriately challenged. Work with your colleagues to enrich your school curriculum to give even weight to each subject, including arts, music, physical activity, social studies, and so on. Teach your students about multiple intelligences and make sure they understand that talent and success come in a variety of forms. Use cooperative learning methods in teaching because they often include elements that engage, encourage, and enable all kinds of students to be active and have a sense of belonging.

Finland has a long history of systematic work to enhance educational equity. As you can see in these suggestions for different leadership levels, collective and multilevel coordinated actions are necessary. Education, health, youth, and social experts need to be on the same page to make sure that all children are supported and helped in a timely manner and offered appropriate assistance. Finland also has a long tradition of public-sector policy coordination that has built coherence at the level of service delivery. Moreover, the Finnish experience suggests that combining all the ideas to improve schools that are presented in this book would have a stronger impact on equity in education. The absence of cross-sector coordination can become an obstacle to having a properly functioning system that improves equity in schools.

CHAPTER

4

Avoid Urban Legends About Finnish Schools

Interest in international borrowing and lending of educational ideas sometimes leads to wrong conclusions and inappropriate expectations regarding the power of those borrowed ideas (Waldow, 2017). There are several incorrect ideas about what Finnish education is and what it isn't that can be very harmful if not understood properly. Many people who saw Michael Moore's film *Where to Invade Next* probably remember that the biggest lesson from the Finnish schools to America was "No Homework." Many people also have concluded that Finnish children have school days that are shorter than elsewhere. Then there are those who believe that Finland's educational excellence is the result of the country's lack of cultural or ethnic diversity. It's no wonder that people tout what's become known as the Finnish miracle in education: What else but a miracle could explain schools with no homework, short school days, but strong academic performance?

A persisting belief around the world is that Finland has the luxury to recruit all its teachers from the top 10 percent of the academic talent pool. This has led to the myth that you must be academically one of "the best and the brightest" if you wish to become a teacher in Finland. Some people have used this myth to justify Teach for America and other fast-track teacher preparation models. These models recruit graduates from top colleges under the assumption that academic ability compensates for a lack of professional preparation, allowing participants to become great teachers. Let me debunk this myth for you.

THE BEST STUDENTS ARE NOT ALWAYS THE BEST TEACHERS

When my niece was finishing upper-secondary school in Finland, more than anything else she wanted to become a primary school teacher. Despite her genuine interest in teaching, she was not successful in getting into the teacher education program at the University of Helsinki that spring. She was smart, played piano, and danced, yet not deemed qualified.

She was not an outlier. Finnish universities regularly turn away applicants like her, forcing them to try again or to study something else. In fact, Finnish primary school teacher education programs that lead to an advanced, research-based degree are so popular among young Finns that only 1 in 10 applicants is accepted each year (Hammerness et al., 2017). Those lucky ones then study five to six years and earn a master's degree in education before they are able to teach a class of their own in primary school.

Some people believe that it is the tough race to become a teacher in Finland that is a key to good teaching and student achievement. Because only 10 percent of applicants pass the rigorous admission system, the story goes, the secret is to recruit new teachers from the top decile of the available candidate pool. This has led some governments and organizations to find new ways to get top students into the teaching profession. Fast-track teacher preparation initiatives have proliferated with the goal of luring smart, young university graduates to teach for a few years. Smarter people make better teachers, or do they?

Who exactly are those who were chosen to become primary school teachers in Finland ahead of my niece? Let's take a closer look at the academic profile distribution of the first-year cohort of students who were selected to begin the teacher education program at the University of Helsinki in the fall of 2014 (what would be the class of 2019 in the United States). The entrance test has two phases. First, all students must first take a national written test called VAKAVA, which is same for all applicants (see Hammerness et al., 2017). Then the best performers on that test—three times the number of those admitted—are invited to the second phase, to take the university-specific aptitude test. At the University of Helsinki, 60 percent of the 120 students accepted to the program were selected based on a combination of their score on the entrance test and their points on the Matriculation Examination that they must take to complete their upper-secondary education; 40 percent of students were awarded a place in the program based solely on their score on the entrance test.

In the spring of 2014, 2,300 students took the VAKAVA national written test, to compete for those 120 available slots at the University of Helsinki. Based on the students' Matriculation Examination results, they were awarded between 1 and 100 points. Students who did very well in Mother Tongue, Mathematics, Foreign Languages, History, Biology, and other subjects on the Matriculation Examination received points ranging from 80 to 100. We can now look at the percentages of successful applicants in different deciles of the academic ability scale. As shown in Figure 4, one-fourth of the accepted students came from the top 20 percent academic ability and another quarter came from the bottom half. This means that half of the first-year students came from the 51–80 points range of measured academic ability; in other words, they can be called academically average students. The final selection of students to the teacher education programs was based not on their academic performance but primarily on other merits, such as communication, teamwork, personality, and overall fit to the teaching

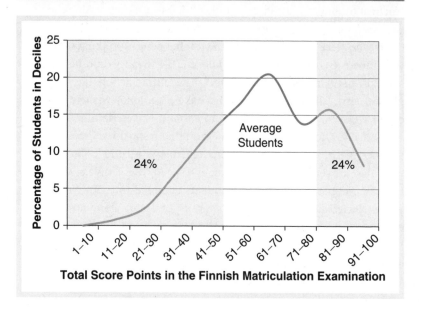

Figure 4 Distribution of Academic Profiles of Students Accepted to the University of Helsinki's Primary School Teacher Education Program in 2014

Total Score Points in the Finnish Matriculation Examination

profession. Therefore, the selection of the primary school teacher education cohort clearly shows that recruitment of "the best and the brightest" into the teaching profession in Finland is a myth.

If Finnish teacher educators thought that teacher quality correlated with measured academic ability, they would have admitted my niece and many of her peers with superior academic records and other merits. Indeed, Finnish universities could easily pick the top academic performers out of the large pool of young talent each year, and all of their new primary school teacher students would have had admirable grades. But they don't because they know that teaching potential is hidden across a range of different types of people. Young athletes, musicians, and youth leaders, for example, often have emerging characteristics of great teachers without strong academic records in school. What Finland shows is that rather than recruiting the academically best young people into teaching, it is better to design initial teacher education in a way that will get the best out of young people who have a passion to teach for life.

The teaching profession has become a fashionable topic among education reformers around the world. In the United States, England, and Australia, policymakers from former U.S. education secretary Arne Duncan to former British prime minister David Cameron have argued that the way to improve education is to attract smarter people to be teachers. International organizations such as the OECD, the World Bank, and McKinsey & Company and prominent corporate leaders such as Michael Barber, former chief education adviser to Pearson, and former New York City schools chancellor Joel Klein, now a board member of Rupert Murdoch's News Corporation, have all claimed that the quality of an education system cannot exceed the quality of its teachers. The myth that claims that the quality of education would boom if only (academically) smarter people taught in schools should not be used to develop education policies. There are, however, evidence-informed education policies and reforms that the United States might consider importing from Finland.

A good step forward would be to admit that the academically strongest students are not necessarily the best teachers. Successful education systems are more concerned about finding the *right* people who will then be properly educated to become career-long teachers. I taught mathematics and science for many years in school. I argue that it was easier for me to understand—and accept—why some students found certain topics and concepts difficult to learn because I was not super-talented in mathematics when I was in school. I also had first-hand experience with what it takes to overcome such challenges in learning mathematics. If you never had to struggle or work hard to learn, then it might be more difficult to understand what would help your students to learn. Oh, and what happened to my niece? She applied again and succeeded. She graduated recently and will be a teacher for life, like most of her university classmates.

FINLAND IS NOT SCRAPPING CURRICULUM SUBJECTS

Another myth was born more recently. In 2015, *The Independent*, one of the United Kingdom's trusted newspapers, reported that Finland was going to replace the teaching of classic school subjects such as mathematics, history, and English with broader, cross-cutting "topics" as part of a major education reform that was launched in August 2016 (Garner, 2015). I have urged readers to stay calm: Despite the reforms, Finnish schools will continue to teach mathematics, history, arts, music, and other subjects in the future.

With the new basic school curriculum introduced in 2014, the school year for all children will include periods during which they look at broader topics, such as climate change, the European Community, or 100 years of Finland's independence, which would bring in multidisciplinary modules on languages, geography, sciences, economics, and other subject areas.

It is important to underline two fundamental peculiarities of the Finnish education system in order to see the real picture. First, education governance is highly decentralized, giving Finland's 311 municipalities a significant amount of freedom to arrange schooling in response to local circumstances. The central government issues legislation, tops up local funding of schools, and provides a guiding framework for what schools should teach and how. Second, Finland's National Core Curriculum (NCC) 2014 for basic schools is a loose common standard that steers curriculum planning at the level of the municipalities and their schools (National Board of Education, 2016). It leaves educators free to find the best ways to offer strong instruction and help all children learn. Therefore, practices vary from school to school and are often customized to local needs and situations.

NCC 2014 is a binding document that sets the overall goals of schooling, describes the principles of teaching and learning, and provides the guidelines for special education, well-being, support services, and student assessment in schools. The concept of "phenomenon-based" teaching—a move away from teaching individual subjects and toward interdisciplinary topics—will have a central place in the new NCC 2014. The term *phenomenon-based teaching* is commonly used in Finland now. The concepts of *problem-based learning* and *project-based teaching*, which are easier to understand and well established in international discourse, may be more useful in explaining Finland's effort to integrate school subjects and ground them in real-life situations.

Integration of subjects and a holistic approach to teaching and learning are not new in Finland. Since the 1980s, Finnish schools have experimented with this approach, and it has been part of the culture of teaching in many Finnish schools since then. This new reform will bring more changes to Finnish middle school subject teachers who have traditionally worked more on their own subjects than together with their peers in school.

What changed in 2016 when NCC 2014 rolled out in all schools is that basic schools for students ages 7–16 years must have at least one extended period of multidisciplinary, problem-based teaching and learning in their curricula. The length of this period is to be decided by schools or agreed upon by local education authorities. Helsinki, the nation's capital and largest local school system, has decided to require two such periods each year that must include all subjects and all students in every school in the city.

Some schools in Helsinki have already arranged teaching in a cross-disciplinary way; other schools will have two or more periods of a few weeks each dedicated to integrated teaching and learning. In most comprehensive schools in other parts of Finland, students will probably have one "project" when they study some of their traditional subjects in a holistic manner. One education chief of a mid-size city in Finland predicted that the end result of this reform will be 300 local variations of the NCC 2014 and that 90% of them probably look a lot like what the schools are doing today. What most advocates of this initiative underestimate is the complexity of implementing problem-based learning in schools in a way that actively engages all students and every teacher. The local control that characterizes education governance in Finland will therefore create numerous ways to implement the new core curriculum rather than make all schools follow the same pedagogical pattern.

KEEP THE FOCUS ON STUDENTS' NEEDS, NOT INTERNATIONAL TEST RANKINGS

You may wonder why Finland's education authorities now insist that all schools must spend time on integration and problem-based teaching when Finnish students' test scores have been declining in the most recent international tests (OECD, 2016b). The answer is that *educators in Finland think that schools should teach what young people need in their lives rather than try to bring national test scores back to where they were.*

Many Finns argue that Finnish youth need more integrated knowledge and skills about real-world issues. Based on the experience of schools that have long used an integrated, problem-based approach, this approach enhances teacher collaboration in schools and makes learning more meaningful to students.

What most stories about Finland's current education reform have failed to cover is the most surprising aspect of the reforms. NCC 2014 states that students must be involved in the planning of problem-based study periods and that they must have a voice in assessing what they have learned from them. Some teachers in Finland see the NCC reforms as a threat and the wrong way to improve teaching and learning in schools. Other teachers think that breaking down the dominance of traditional subjects and isolation of teaching is an opportunity to create more fundamental change in schools.

How have Finnish authorities reacted to the recent downturn in the country's PISA results? The response to a drop in test scores in some countries would be to allocate more time and resources to teaching the subjects that are tested and in which scores have fallen. In some other countries, education ministers and other education leaders have elevated the importance of international tests, including PISA (Sellar et al., 2017), by insisting that schools taking part in these tests must take them seriously and do their very best. There are, as we have seen, many ways to do that.

Finland has taken none of these steps. Indeed, doing well in PISA has never been a target in Finnish policies. Instead, education policies now focus on enhancing arts, music, and physical education for all students in every school, hoping that would improve student engagement in school. Since 2016, all schools have been required to include one hour of physical activity for all children every day. Time to play in and out of school is also emphasized as a critical element of learning, well-being, and health. As described earlier, Finland's current school curriculum reform shifts pedagogical emphasis from teaching subjects, including reading, mathematics, and science, toward more integrated, problem-based learning.

The Comenius' Oath

As a teacher I am engaged in educating the next generation, which is one of the most important human tasks. My aim in this will be to renew and pass on the existing reserve of human knowledge, culture, and skills.

I undertake to act with justice and fairness in all that I do and to promote the development of my pupils and students, so that each individual may grow up as a complete human being in accordance with his or her aptitudes and talents.

I will also strive to assist parents, guardians, and others responsible for working with children and young people in their educational functions.

I will not reveal information that is communicated to me confidentially, and I will respect the privacy of children and young people. I will also protect their physical and psychological inviolability.

I will endeavor to shield the children and young people in my care from political and economic exploitation and defend the rights of every individual to develop his or her own religious and political convictions.

(Continued)

I will make continuous efforts to maintain and develop my professional skills, committing myself to the common goals of my profession and to the support of my colleagues in their work. I will act in the best interests of the community at large and strive to strengthen the esteem in which the teaching profession is held.

Source: OAJ (Finnish Trade Union of Education). Comenius' Oath. Retrieved from http://www.oaj.fi/cs/oaj/Comeniuksen%20valan%20vannominen.

Ways to Move Forward

It would be foolish to imitate an education system under any circumstances, and it would be catastrophic to try to pull together an education system based on myths from other education systems. Here are concrete ideas for education system leaders and for all school leaders, inspired by actual practices and policies in Finland.

1. *System leaders: Strengthen the teaching profession by devising an ethical pledge for all teachers similar to the Hippocratic oath taken by physicians or the Comenius Oath taken by Finnish teachers.*

   Design this teachers' oath so that it aims to enhance teachers' status in society and remind every teacher that the teaching profession is important and includes values, principles, and rights that teachers must respect. If you phrase this pledge so that it emphasizes fairness, equality, dignity, and professionalism in all actions that teachers do alone and together with one another, it may help in raising ethical standards and implementing other important ideas in your schools. Establish a common procedure for taking the oath and use it consistently in public events for teachers. The Comenius' Oath is an initiative launched by the Trade Union of Education in Finland in 2017 (see box).

2. *Principals: Launch an annual Day of Failure*

   Introduce in your annual work plans a day for recognizing risk-taking, creativity, and innovation. If you dare, call it the Day of Failure. The focus of that day should be the fact that "only those who dare to fail greatly can ever achieve greatly," as Robert F. Kennedy said. Invite entrepreneurs, business leaders, and scientists to speak about their work and the role of learning from failures. Help teachers to show students that failure is part of successful learning rather than something that should be avoided. Make sure that all students are involved in planning and implementing these days. Follow up to see if the Day of Failure affects the ways you perceive your leadership work. Finland recognizes the annual Day of Failure on October 13.

Epilogue

Intentional Dessert

The international conference in upstate New York that began with my meeting with George Pataki was just about to end, concluding with a dinner for attendees and speakers. The conference had discussed, among other topics, the pros and cons of using global learning metrics to raise the quality of education around the world. I shared a table with some school and district leaders and businesspeople from the United States. "Is it true that PISA was invented in Finland?" they asked. "Why do you think so?" I wanted to know. "Well, there are some speculations that PISA measures student achievement that fits to the Finnish version of teaching and curriculum," came the response. I said that this is a really interesting question because very few people actually know why the OECD is the host of the most influential international learning metric. To shed more light on this intriguing question, I offered the following story.

HOW PISA WAS BORN

The origin of PISA dates to the 1980s. A report commissioned by President Ronald Reagan's administration, called *A Nation at Risk,* had spelled out strongly, although based on flawed statistical analysis and conclusions, that the K–12 school system in the United States was in crisis and, therefore, a fundamental change of course was needed. The International Association for the Evaluation of Educational Achievement (IEA) has carried out comparative studies of students' achievement in mathematics, science, and reading literacy since the 1960s, and the United States has taken part in these studies, which primarily served research purposes. Reporting back to the participating countries took so long that education policymakers, especially those in the United States, insisted that there must be a faster way to administer these international studies. They also concluded that because education in the United States is under the control of states and individual school districts, Washington, D.C., needed an organization like the OECD to help provide comparable international data about the performance of the American education system. The main rationale was to use internationally comparable evidence from the most developed countries to prove the poor condition of the American school system and thereby justify the call for action—seven-hour school days, standardized testing, and merit-based pay for teachers—outlined in *A Nation at Risk*.

In the 1980s, however, the OECD was not ready to start testing schoolchildren in its member countries, because at that time the OECD's education unit had only a handful of staff. The United States was pushing the OECD hard on this matter, so hard that in a meeting in 1987 it threatened to resign from the organization—as it had from the United Nations Educational, Scientific and Cultural Organisation (UNESCO) in 1984—if the OECD did not respond to its demand to generate internationally comparable data about student achievement. The OECD had no choice but to begin to seek ways to make its wealthiest member happy.

Support for the United States on this issue came from an unexpected fellow member. France, the host country of the OECD, was under political control from the other side of the political aisle than the United States. Socialist French governments of the 1980s were upset with the elitist nature of the French education system created by a previous bourgeois political power that did not provide equal opportunities to all but only to the crème de la crème in French society. Their plan was to reform the entire education system by enhancing equality of opportunity and weakening the link between children's family background and their educational success. France stepped forward to support the initiative made by the Americans, but with political interests opposite those of their American colleagues. French politicians also needed internationally comparable and trustworthy evidence to show the poor quality of the French elitist education system so that they would have reason to introduce education reforms for more equal and inclusive education.

The political climate inside the OECD was ready for a radical, new initiative that would measure what 15 year olds in OECD member countries know and are able to do with what they have learned in reading literacy, mathematics, and science in school. In 1995, Tom Alexander, British director of the OECD's education department, presented the blueprint for the new international student assessment to the representatives of the OECD member states. Many attendees of that meeting didn't like Alexander's idea to test students at the end of the lower secondary stage (when they were about 15 years of age), although others argued that this is the age when many young people are finishing compulsory schooling and moving to the upper secondary level. After two years of lobbying, a majority of OECD member countries finally accepted the new role that the OECD would have through PISA. Some countries, including Finland, remained unconvinced that this is what the OECD should do. Nevertheless, the strange alliance of conservative republicans of the New World and the socialist left-wingers of Old Europe led to a process that in the dawn of the new millennium surprised several countries. But both the United States and France accomplished their missions with PISA—their performance was below the international average.

This was all very interesting to my colleagues around the table. But how has the OECD's PISA influenced education policies and reforms around the world?

INFLUENCE OF PISA

The first PISA results were released in Paris on December 4, 2001. Expectations among most of the participants—twenty-eight member and four other countries that time—were high. Many countries believed that their education system would be ranked among the very best in this first-ever international student assessment focusing on knowledge and skills commonly required in emerging new global economies. England, Scotland, Germany, Sweden, the Netherlands, Australia, New Zealand, and the United States were all seen as international models that others tried to imitate. Andreas Schleicher, one of the architects of PISA, remembers that in the meetings of the senior education authorities from the OECD member countries, many delegates reported how innovations and radical reforms in their countries were supposed to lead to stellar outcomes. Enthusiasm among the Finns and some others was much more modest. Humorously, the Finns said that if Finland does better than its western neighbor Sweden, they would be happy. At that time, there already were many signs of emerging global competition for top spots in the new emerging global education ranking.

News regarding the findings of the first OECD PISA in 2001 surprised many. In reading literacy, which was the primary focus of the 2000 PISA study, the top OECD achievers were Finland, Canada, New Zealand, Australia, and Ireland. Educators in Germany, Switzerland, the United Kingdom, Denmark, Norway, and Sweden were shocked, not only by the new "big five" in education but also because their educational performance lagged so far behind the lead pack. Interestingly, Finland and other Nordic countries seemed to have the most equitable school systems in the sense that in these countries children's family background explained less of student achievement, and performance differences among schools were smaller than in other countries.

"How did the Finns react to the news? With a national celebration of victory? Fanfares and fireworks?" my American colleagues around the table asked. "Nothing like that," I replied. I told them that the news came at a time when there was growing domestic criticism concerning the quality and overall relevance of Finland's nine-year basic school, as I describe in *Finnish Lessons 2.0* (Sahlberg, 2015). Scores of business leaders, many academicians (especially in mathematics and sciences), and some politicians had expressed their dissatisfaction with the current state of schooling. Some were urging Finland to adopt new policies and practices that would increase flexibility, allow early specialization, encourage more competition between schools, and expand parental choice in education. They argued that global economic competition, expanding European labor markets, and emerging new digital technologies required better educated people with more specialized knowledge and skills than Finland's old school system was able to generate. The first PISA results revealed that many of these accusations against the school system contradicted the international evidence.

THE AFTERMATH OF THE FIRST PISA

After several months of international media coverage about the new world order in education, Finland's reaction was twofold. First, some observers in Finland thought that there must be something wrong because Finland, which employs no standardized tests, was ranked number one on a standardized student assessment. At the same time, an increasing number of countries—for example, England, Australia, and many parts of the United States—were focusing increasingly on core subjects and frequently testing student achievement through standardized tests.

The second reaction was that perhaps the OECD made a measuring mistake or incorrectly computed the statistical calculations that lifted Finland from the international average to the top. This perception was reinforced by comments from some upper–secondary school teachers and university professors claiming that the overall level of academic abilities of enrolling students had been in steady decline since the 1980s. An absence of systematic research on the success (or failure) of education reforms and related data about performance trends of schools and students led to an obvious conclusion: Let's wait until the 2003 PISA results are published to be clear on Finland's true position vis-à-vis other education systems.

Three years later, 41 countries (or economies) participated in the 2003 PISA, which this time focused on mathematics. The OECD top five were Finland, South Korea, Japan, the Netherlands, and Canada. At the same time, the United States, Australia, New Zealand, and Sweden were on a downward trend in their students' mathematics achievement compared to the result three years earlier (England's results were rejected from this PISA cycle due to sampling error). Now there began to be more general acceptance in Finland that there is something unique in the Finnish school system (in addition to cultural homogeneity and size) that the Finns had realized before most others. Besides the reports that Finnish PISA coordinators published, there was little information on why the Finnish school system was performing better than many others. The 2006 PISA had science as the major subject area and 55 countries and economies taking part. After results became public in December 2007, showing Finland, Canada, Japan, New Zealand, and Australia leading the OECD countries, Finland become the international rock star in education. It was not only the high student achievement in reading, mathematics, and science that made Finland internationally famous; it also had the most equitable school system of all the OECD countries.

We had finished our desserts, but the conversation continued. "What has been the significance of the OECD's PISA study internationally?" a woman asked. She claimed that some experts believe that PISA has done more harm than good with regard to improving education systems, whereas others say that some international benchmarks are needed for developing education systems in the right direction.

PISA'S GLOBAL NARRATIVES

Whatever your view, PISA has created two important and interesting global narratives of educational change.

Narrative #1: The Criteria of Success

The first narrative is the lessons learned from *successful education systems* that are built on international, comparative analysis of education systems that perform well in four criteria of success: quality of student achievement, equity of outcomes, participation and completion rates in various levels of education, and economic efficiency of the education system. Based on these criteria, the most successful OECD school systems at the time of writing include Canada, Estonia, Japan, the Netherlands, and Finland.

Narrative #2: Global Educational Reform Movement

The second global narrative is about common trends in education policies and reforms in countries that have performed below expectations. Soon after the first PISA study, policymakers and researchers began to wonder why the countries that were thought to be more successful in terms of quality and equity of education outcomes performed consistently worse than predicted. Was it because they didn't have something that the more successful education systems had in their schools or societies? Maybe high-performing school systems just did some critical things in education better than others? Or was there an education reform paradigm that dominated these lower-performers that simply was based on the wrong policy drivers? I have called this international agenda that typically builds on competition, parental choice, standardization, accountability, and privatization the Global Educational Reform Movement (GERM); it is described in detail in my other publications (Sahlberg, 2015, 2016).

There is not much research yet on the normative effects of the OECD's PISA study on national education policies and reforms. The OECD commissioned an external evaluation to estimate PISA's relevance, effectiveness, and sustainability and its impact on participating countries. This review revealed that PISA had more influence in national education policies than local or school-level practices (OECD, 2012). It also concluded that the influence of PISA on policy was increasing over time. PISA has had the most significant impact on countries that experienced lower-than-expected performance in the first two or three PISA studies from 2000 to 2006. Germany, Denmark, and Japan were among those countries in which PISA had a significant role in modifying national education policies (Breakspear, 2015; Sellar et al., 2017). Germany and Japan sent several high-level delegations to investigate the Finnish school system, whereas similar delegations from Denmark visited

Finland much less frequently. Germany tried to test Finland's comprehensive school structure, which educates all students within the same school type without early selection, in some of its states but without notable success. Japan adopted Finland's method of reading instruction—called the PISA method—in some schools in Tokyo and Kyoto. Interestingly, it has taken much longer for policymakers in the United States and England to realize that the Finnish education system can offer inspiration. England has been especially persistent, even stubborn, in downplaying the Finnish experience.

U.S. RESPONSE TO PISA

The conference dinner was almost over, but one important issue had not yet been discussed. My dinner-mates asked, "What has been the influence of the Finnish education system in the United States?"

It has become a common practice in national policymaking in most OECD countries and in many nonmember countries to use PISA results to identify successful education systems. OECD (2012) summarizes Finland's international education policy impact like this:

> The education policies of Finland have been cited most broadly across countries/economies, signaling that, through its performance in PISA, Finland is regarded as a key source for cross-national policy learning and borrowing. (p. 28)

After the 2009 PISA results were released, the U.S. Department of Education, led at the time by Arne Duncan, invited the National Center on Education and the Economy (NCEE) to prepare a report on behalf of the OECD, answering the question: "What are the lessons from PISA to the United States?" (OECD, 2011). In this analysis, Finland had a central role as a source of ideas for the United States; however, there has been much more interest in Finland's education system at the school and district levels than at the state and federal levels.

In response to my dinner-mates' question, I said that I distinguished three types of effects that Finland's system has had in general, including in the United States:

1. Finland's education system has inspired experiments to improve education in American schools. Examples include increasing recess in the Dallas–Fort Worth, Texas, area; honoring teachers and loosening the grip of standardized testing in West Virginia; and improving science education in Orange County, California. In 2017, American primary school teacher Tim Walker, who lives and teaches in Finland, published a book-length repertoire of pedagogical ideas and models based on his first-hand experience as a teacher in Helsinki, titled *Teach Like Finland: 33 Simple Strategies for Joyful Classrooms*.

2. Finnish education has shaped and facilitated the dialogue on teacher policies in the United States. Analysts of the highest performing education systems have recognized that one feature common to all of these education systems is that they have teacher policies that focus on initial teacher education; supporting, valuing, and trusting teachers in their work; and arranging systematic access to professional learning and development throughout their careers. Firing bad teachers through punitive teacher evaluations and replacing them through fast-track teacher training initiatives are absent in Finland and other successful education systems. In other words, higher performing education systems cultivate and protect teacher professionalism and leadership better than others.

   Finland is known for its advanced academic, research-based teacher education. It is one of the most popular fields of higher education among young Finns. International conferences, handbooks, and networks on the teaching profession regularly include insights from Finnish teacher education. In this regard, there has been a notable influence from Finnish teacher education and teacher policy models in the United States. For example, several research projects led by Stanford

University, such as the International Teacher Policy Study (Hammerness et al., 2017), have included teacher education scholars from Finland. Publications by Linda Darling-Hammond regularly discuss aspects of teacher education in Finland (Darling-Hammond, 2015; Darling-Hammond & Lieberman, 2012). Finnish teacher policies have inspired debates in the United States concerning the selectivity and content of teacher education programs as well as the need for continuous professional learning and development.

3. The Finnish education system has inspired other countries to open model schools based on Finnish educational philosophy and pedagogy. Most education experts admit that it is impossible to transfer the Finnish school model from Finland to other countries. Trust in local education authorities and professional autonomy of teachers in Finland are examples of cultural features that don't travel well from Finland to other countries. Regardless of the conditions that limit exporting of the Finnish school model to other countries, there have been efforts to do so but without notable success.

Ways to Move Forward

Experienced international educators accept the fact that we can always learn from other countries no matter how different they are from our own. This book has shown that Finland's educational success has been possible because the Finns have been open to other countries' ideas and models to improve their schools. The way to move forward in the United States is therefore built on the same assumption that, regardless of the many differences between the two countries, Finland can inspire American educators and policymakers to think differently about what they do in many ways. Here are three such ideas for system leaders, principals, and teachers.

1. *System leaders: Establish better understanding of the Global Learning Metrics*

   Review the research literature on international large-scale assessments (also known as Global Learning Metrics), such as

PISA, the Trends in International Mathematics and Science Study (TIMSS), and the Progress in International Reading Literacy Study (PIRLS). Identify the assumptions and limitations of these assessments, especially regarding their power to predict the quality of different school systems. Engage your middle and high school leaders in conversations that aim at better understanding of how these assessments can be used to help your schools. Read *The Global Education Race: Taking the Measure of PISA and International Testing* by Sam Sellar, Greg Thompson, and David Rutkowski (2017) to deepen conversation about international large-scale assessments. Communicate what you have learned to political leaders and citizens in your community.

2. *Principals: Be a leading learner in your school*

Engage your teachers in an ongoing dialogue regarding school reform and learn together with them about what works in other countries' education systems. Determine what your school's goals are, whether they are limited to student academic achievement or whether they include other goals related to equity, student engagement and well-being, or school culture. Use this book to inspire teachers to consider how you together could strengthen the role of play in your school, how to collect and use more small data in school improvement, and how to enhance equity in your school and district.

3. *Teachers: Connect internationally*

Find international networks of schools or teachers that act in your area of interest. Build relationships with your colleagues in other countries through these networks. Work with your colleagues in your own school and with those in other countries to implement one or two methods in your school that will gather small data so that incremental changes and adjustments can be made at the individual student level to enhance student success. I mention three examples of international networks in the Conclusion chapter that follows.

Conclusion

Don't Be Denied

FinnishED Leadership is about the need to build deeper professionalism and create more collaborative cultures in and around our schools. This book speaks for lateral learning between one teacher and another, one school and another, one district and another, and one nation and another. It also suggests blending the best ideas of the past with opportunities and a vision of the future. Educational leadership in Finland, in schools, in districts, and at the national level, is about balancing hard evidence and storytelling—or big data and small data. Hard evidence includes figures in international studies, numbers in national assessments, statistics in national databases, and research findings that inform education authorities and school leaders about the state of the education system. Storytelling is often about personal observations, informal interactions, and focused experiences found in classrooms, schools, and communities. Stories from other school leaders can tell us a lot about how to move forward in our own school settings.

FOCUSING ON VISIBLE AND PERMANENT IMPROVEMENT

I have chosen the four ideas for this book intentionally so that when well implemented in structures and cultures of school, they will provide visible and permanent improvements in your school. Some of the ideas here are easier to put in practice than others. Enhancing resiliency and equity of learning outcomes in your school or district is probably the most demanding undertaking of the suggestions in this book. Indeed, there is a significant difference between increasing recess and enhancing equity in terms of the complexity of the issues and the agency of school leaders.

I believe that, regardless of these complexities in enhancing educational equity in schools, there are many things that can and should be done now. Smarten school curricula by having it address curiosity, risk-taking, multiple intelligences, play, and whole-child pedagogies across the school in coherent ways. Successful educational change process is a function of shaping and fine-tuning good ideas as they gradually build leadership capacity, teacher agency, and ownership.

The relatively good performance of the education system in Finland is a result of a network of interrelated factors. Finland managed, as I have written in *Finnish Lessons 2.0* (Sahlberg, 2015), to build a well-performing education system by enhancing the culture of schools based on collaboration, professionalism, shared purpose, focused strategy, long-term implementation, and interdependency of different public-sector policies. When you move forward with the ideas presented in this book, remember that to rush educational improvement is to ruin it.

WHERE TO LOOK NEXT

If you find ideas in this book helpful, then you would probably also like to learn more about international innovation networks that aim to improve collaborative cultures and share leading practices between schools and education systems. HundrED is a new education initiative to celebrate Finland's 100th anniversary in 2017.[1] Its mission is to find and share inspiring innovations in K–12 education around the world, not only in Finland. In the lead-up to Finland's centenary in December 2017, HundrED is creating 100 case studies of the most exciting education ideas worldwide and testing them in selected schools. These innovations can be small, classroom-level projects, or system-wide policies and programs. The key criterion is that they should have potential to change education, and should be scalable and replicable by others. The case studies will be in the

---

1. See the HundrED website at https://hundred.org/en.

public domain for teachers and leaders to use freely. HundrED is just one example of efforts to break the barriers between leading practices and those hungry for ideas that can change education.

Other examples include New Pedagogies for Deep Learning (NPDL), which includes seven countries: Australia, Canada, Finland, the Netherlands, New Zealand, Uruguay, and the United States; the Atlantic Rim Collaboratory (ARC), which is a network of eight education systems: Aruba, California, Finland, Iceland, Ireland, Ontario, Scotland, and Vermont; and the Finland-Alberta (FINAL) Partnership (Alberta Teachers' Association, 2016). See the box for more on these collaborations.

International Collaborations

What Is NPDL?

New Pedagogies for Deep Learning (NPDL) is an international partnership of 1,000 schools in 10 countries. It is based on clusters and networks of schools building knowledge and practices that develop deep learning and foster whole-system change. The NPDL organization works alongside educators to change the role of teachers to that of activators of learning who design learning experiences that build on learner strengths and needs; create new knowledge using real-life problem solving; and help all students identify their talents, purpose, and passion. NPDL assumes that every student deserves to learn deeply, and it supports whole systems—schools, provinces, states, and countries—to take action, make a positive impact, and grasp opportunities that will lead to success in life. It is a community of families, teachers, school leaders, and policy makers worldwide who are seeking ways to transform pedagogies and provide the conditions that will facilitate deep learning.

The Vision of ARC

The vision of the Atlantic Rim Collaboratory (ARC) is to establish a global group of educational systems that advances equity, excellence, well-being, inclusion, democracy, and human rights for all students within high-quality, professionally run systems. In a world

(Continued)

(Continued)

of disruptive economic transformations, growing inequalities and rapid change, it is important to broaden and deepen our approach to how we interpret and improve high-quality educational systems for all our students. ARC works in a way that complements the international initiatives of transnational organizations like the United Nations and the OECD. It also advances a broad vision of educational excellence that embraces issues such as special education inclusion, many kinds of diversity, and wellness supports within systems that build and promote a strong and sustainable teaching profession. ARC builds on the current strengths and strategies of participating educational systems with the intention of improving them over time through deliberately designed processes. It will seek out and spread current best practices, develop next practices that reflect ARC values, and cultivate collective responsibility for shared success and global impact. ARC will energize member systems with agendas determined by themselves; stimulate ideas by providing high-level contact with thought leaders; widen and deepen global narratives of educational change; and lead to clear, collectively determined outcomes.

Finland-Alberta Partnership (FINAL)

The Finland-Alberta (FINAL) partnership between Alberta and Finnish schools enables principals, teachers, other school staff, and students from preschool to general upper secondary and vocational schools to examine ways to improve their schools through collaborative inquiry and development activities. The program includes short teaching assignments, job shadowing, and student projects focused on addressing shared concerns about creating better schools. FINAL is for those who wish to make a positive impact in their schools. The partnership was initiated in 2011 with the theme "a great school for all," which connects to the research study *A Great School for All: Transforming Education in Alberta*. Through FINAL, which has been funded by the Ministry of Education and Culture in Finland and the Alberta Teachers' Association, about 25 schools in Finland and Alberta have been partnering with one another.

Sources: NPDL website, http://npdl.global; ARC website, www.atlantic rimcollaboratory.org/; Atlantic Rim Collaboratory (2017); Alberta Teachers' Association (2016).

Sir Winston Churchill said: "You can always count on Americans to do the right thing—after they've tried everything else." American educators have understood the irony of this adage very well. Successful education systems—such as those in Canada, the Netherlands, Singapore, and Finland—employ almost orthogonal education policies in their education system improvement strategies: collaboration rather than competition between schools, creativity and flexibility more than standardization and alignment, teacher and leader professionalism instead of allowing schools to employ nonprofessional staff, and trust in teachers more than punitive accountability. But it doesn't have to be this way in the United States any longer. International benchmarking and new international networks' deeper analysis of smart practices have provided evidence-based case studies showing their impact around the world. The fact of the matter is that there are hundreds of inspiring examples of educational innovation in the United States that have potential to change the world of education visibly and permanently in the United States and beyond.

I hope this book has convinced you that you can learn from promising practices in other countries to help you improve what you do. This book also argues that necessary knowledge and models to significantly improve American schools already exist somewhere in the nation's 100,000 schools and therefore better implementation of those ideas should be put before the addiction to innovate. As an educational leader, you should also be a leading learner in your school or district. Today, 80 percent of innovations in the business sector come from customers and citizen developers, not from researchers or test laboratories. Research mechanisms are too slow to feed new ideas to rapidly developing markets. Education systems also evolve fast. One more time: most leading ideas and innovations in education are already in use somewhere. The education leader's task is to find them, learn them, and put them into practice if there is reason to believe they will work. That is the grand idea of this book.

References

Abrams, S. (2016). *Education and the commercial mindset*. Cambridge, MA: Harvard University Press.

Adamson, F., Åstrand, B., & Darling-Hammond, L. (Eds.) *Global education reform: How privatization and public investment influence education outcomes*. New York: Routledge.

American Academy of Pediatrics. (2013). Policy statement: The crucial role of recess in school. *Pediatrics, 131*(1), 183–188.

Alberta Teachers' Association. (2016). *ATA Magazine*, 97(1).

Atlantic Rim Collaboratory. (2017). *ARC Declarations*. http://atrico.org/data/uploads/2017/01/arc-declaration.pdf

Bickham, D. S., Kavanaugh, J. R., Alden, S., & Rich, M. (2015). *The state of play: How play affects developmental outcomes*. Boston: Boston Children's Hospital Center on Media and Child Health.

Breakspear, S. (2015). Measuring How the World Learns: An examination of the OECD's PISA and its uses in national policy evaluation. Unpublished Doctoral Dissertation. University of Cambridge, UK.

Chavez, R. M. (2017, January 19). Remarks at ComputeFest 2017. https://www.youtube.com/watch?v=VF6DrX9H0Ug&list=PLfjZYvoyxDtZGcgBLEW8vWUGocpiMLpSS&index=8

Cope, B., & Kalantzis, M. (2016). Big data comes to school: Implications for learning, assessment, and research. *AERA Open*, (2)2, 1–19. doi:10.1177/2332858416641907

Darling-Hammond, L. (2010). *The flat world and education. How America's commitment to equity will determine our future*. New York: Teachers College Press.

Darling-Hammond, L. (Ed.) (2015). *Teaching in a flat world*. New York: Teachers College Press.

Darling-Hammond, L., & Lieberman, A. (Eds.) (2012). *Teacher education around the world: Practices & policies in high achieving nations*. New York: Routledge.

Doyle, W. (2017). How Finland's youngest learners obey the rules—by fooling around in school. *Hechinger Report*, January 8.

Gardner, H. (1983). *Frames of mind: The theory of multiple intelligences.* New York: Basic Books.

Garner, R. (2015). Finland schools: Subjects scrapped and replaced with 'topics' as country reforms its education system. *The Independent,* March 25.

Hammerness, K., Ahtiainen, R., & Sahlberg, P. (2017). *Empowered educations in Finland. How high-performing systems shape teaching quality.* San Francisco: Jossey-Bass.

Hargreaves, A., & Fullan, M. (2012). *Professional capital: Transforming teaching in every school.* New York: Teachers College Press.

Heckman, J. (2011). The economics of inequality: The value of early childhood education. *American Educator, 35*(1), 31–35.

Howie, E. K., & Pate, R. R. (2012). Physical activity and academic achievement in children: A historical perspective. *Journal of Sport and Health Science, 1*(3), 160–169.

Lego Foundation. (2013). *The future of play. Defining the role and value of play in the 21st century.* Billund, Denmark: Lego Foundation.

Lindstrom, M. (2016). *Small data: Tiny clues that uncover huge trends.* New York: St. Martin's Press.

Merrow, J. (2017). *Addicted to Reform: A 12-step program to rescue public education.* New York: The New Press.

National Board of Education. (2016). *National Core Curriculum for Basic Education 2014.* Helsinki: National Board of Education.

OECD. (2011). *Lessons from PISA for the United States: Strong performers and successful reformers in education.* Paris: OECD Publishing.

OECD. (2012). *The policy impact of Pisa: An exploration of the normative effects of international benchmarking in school system performance.* OECD Education Working Paper #71. Paris: OECD.

OECD. (2016a). *Education at a glance 2016.* Paris: OECD Publishing.

OECD. (2016b). *PISA 2015 results: Excellence and equity in education.* Paris: OECD Publishing.

Quarry, G. (2017). Adrian Piccoli: The education minister who "just gets it." *Education HQ Australia,* January 27. http://au.educationhq.com/news/37877/adrian-piccoli-the-education-minister-who-just-gets-it/

Robert Wood Johnson Foundation (2007). *Recess rules: Why the undervalued playtime may be America's best investment for healthy kids and healthy schools.* Princeton, NJ: RWJ Foundation.

Sahlberg, P. (2015). *Finnish lessons 2.0: What can the world learn from educational change in Finland?* (2nd. ed.). New York: Teachers College Press.

Sahlberg, P. (2016). Global Educational Reform Movement and its impact on teaching. In Mundy, K., Green, A., Lingard, R., & Verger, A. (Eds.),

The handbook of global policy and policymaking in education. New York: Wiley-Blackwell.

Sahlberg, P., & Berry, J. (2003). *Small group learning in school mathematics. Teachers' and pupils' ideas about groupwork in school.* Turku: Finnish Educational Research Association.

Sahlberg, P. and Hargreaves, A. (2015). The Tower of PISA is badly leaning. *Washington Post,* March 24.

Sahlberg, P., & Hasak, J. (2016). 'Big data' was supposed to fix education. It didn't. It's time for 'small data.' *Washington Post,* May 9.

Schleicher, A. (2013). Big data and PISA. *OECD Education and Skills Today,* July 23. http://oecdeducationtoday.blogspot.com/2013/07/big-data-and-pisa.html

Sellar, S., Thompson, G., & Rutkowski, D. (2017). *The global education race: Taking the measure of PISA and international testing.* Edmonton, Alberta, Canada: Brush Education Inc.

SHAPE America. (2017). *Program proves more recess improves academic performance and behavior.* http://50million.shapeamerica.org/program-proves-more-recess-improves-academic-performance-and-behavior/

Sharan, S. (Ed.) (1999). *The handbook of cooperative learning methods.* Westport, CT: Praeger.

Showers, B., & Joyce, B. (1996). The evolution of peer coaching. *Educational Leadership, 53*(6), 12–16.

Shumaker, H. 2016. *It's ok to go up the slide: Renegade rules for raising confident and creative kids.* New York: Tarcher.

Syväoja, H., Kantomaa, M., Laine, K., Jaakkola, T., Pyhältö, K., & Tammelin, T. (2012). *Liikunta ja oppiminen.* Tilannekatsaus lokakuu 2012. Helsinki: Opetushallitus.

Tucker, M. (2012). Why the "market theory" of education reform doesn't work. *Washington Post,* October 12.

Waldow, F. (2017). Projecting images of the "good" and the "bad school": Top scorers in educational large-scale assessments as reference societies. *Compare: A Journal of Comparative and International Education, 47*(1), 1–18.

Walker, T. D. (2017). *Teach like Finland: 33 simple strategies for joyful classrooms.* New York: Norton.

White, R. (2013). *The power of play: Research summary on play and learning.* Minneapolis: Minnesota Children's Museum.

Index

Science, students' attitudes
     toward, 40–42
Sellar, S., 32, 67, 77, 82
Shape America, 24 (box)
Sharan, S., 8
Showers, Beverly, 11
Small Data (Lindstrom), 39
Social issues, 12
Special education
     in Finland, 47, 54
     prioritizing, 56
Standards
     Common Core, 4
     in Finland, 64
Storytelling, 83
Student welfare teams, 37
Subjects
     integration of, 65, 67
     See also Curriculum
Success, criteria of, 76–77
System leaders. *See* Leaders
Syväoja, H., 23

Teacher education
     fast-track, 60
     in Finland, 11, 51 (box), 60–63,
          62 (figure), 79–80
Teachers
     academic strength of, 63
     autonomy of, 43, 80
     blamed for educational failures,
          4, 13
     breaks for, 25
     computers as, 32
     learning for, 10–11, 53
     merit-based pay, 55
     oath for, 67–68 (box), 68
     professional development,
          10–11, 53
     and recess, 27
     relationships with colleagues in
          other countries, 82

respect for, 11
small data and, 36, 39–42,
     43–45, 82
whole-child approach, 57
Teaching, phenomenon-based, 65
Teaching, project-based, 65
Teach Like Finland (Walker), 79
10,000 Steps a Day, 26–27
Tennessee, 19
Testing, international, 32. *See also*
     PISA
Testing, standardized, 4, 30, 53, 55
     in Finland, 37
     focus on, 75
     See also Data, big; PISA
Test scores, focus on, 66
Thompson, G., 32, 82
Time, 15, 17
     in American schools vs. Finnish,
          16–17
     pace of school day, 18–19
Time, instructional, 17
     decreasing, 19
     in Finland, 20, 21 (figure)
Transparency, 29
Trust, lack of, 45
Tucker, M., 55
20-percent rule, 25, 26

United Nations Educational,
     Scientific and Cultural
     Organization (UNESCO), 72

VAKAVA, 61

Waldow, F., 59
Walker, Tim, 79
Where to Invade Next (film), 59
White, R., 19
Whole-child approach, 57
Work loads, student, 18
World Bank, 63

CORWIN
LEADERSHIP

Simon T. Bailey & Marceta F. Reilly
On providing a simple, sustainable framework that will help you move your school from mediocrity to brilliance.

Edie L. Holcomb
Use data to construct an equitable learning environment, develop instruction, and empower effective PL communities.

Debbie Silver & Dedra Stafford
Equip educators to develop resilient and mindful learners primed for academic growth and personal success.

Peter Gamwell & Jane Daly
A fresh perspective on how to nurture creativity, innovation, leadership, and engagement.

Steven Katz, Lisa Ain Dack, & John Malloy
Leverage the oppositional forces of top-down expectations and bottom-up experience to create an intelligent, responsive school.

Lyn Sharratt & Beate Planche
A resource-rich guide that provides a strategic path to achieving sustainable communities of deep learners.

Peter M. DeWitt
Meet stakeholders where they are, motivate them to improve, and model how to do it.

Leadership that Makes an Impact

Charlotte Danielson
Harness the power of informal professional conversation and invite teachers to boost achievement.

Liz Wiseman, Lois Allen, & Elise Foster
Use leadership to bring out the best in others—liberating staff to excel and doubling your team's effectiveness.

Eric Sheninger
Use digital resources to create a new school culture, increase engagement, and facilitate real-time PD.

Russell J. Quaglia, Michael J. Corso, & Lisa L. Lande
Listen to your school's voice to see how you can increase engagement, involvement, and academic motivation.

Michael Fullan, Joanne Quinn, & Joanne McEachen
Learn the right drivers to mobilize complex, coherent, whole-system change and transform learning for all students.

C RWIN LEADERSHIP

CORWIN

A SAGE Publishing Company

Helping educators make the greatest impact

CORWIN HAS ONE MISSION: to enhance education through intentional professional learning.

We build long-term relationships with our authors, educators, clients, and associations who partner with us to develop and continuously improve the best evidence-based practices that establish and support lifelong learning.

Solutions you want. Experts you trust. Results you need.